FROM SUPERMARINE
SEAFIRE XVII
TO DOUGLAS DC-10

*For my wife and family who
endured, and survived,
a mainly absentee husband and father.*

FROM SUPERMARINE
SEAFIRE XVII
TO DOUGLAS DC-10
A Lifetime of Flight

by

Ronald Williams

Pen & Sword
AVIATION

First published in Great Britain in 2012 by
Pen & Sword Aviation
an imprint of
Pen & Sword Books Ltd
47 Church Street
Barnsley
South Yorkshire
S70 2AS

ISBN: 978-1-84884-647-0

A CIP catalogue record for this book is
available from the British Library.

Typeset in 12/13.5pt Palatino by
Concept, Huddersfield, West Yorkshire

Printed and bound in England by
CPI Group (UK) Ltd, Croydon, CRO 4YY

Pen & Sword Books Ltd incorporates the Imprints of Pen & Sword
Aviation, Pen & Sword Family History, Pen & Sword Maritime, Pen &
Sword Military, Pen & Sword Discovery, Wharncliffe Local History,
Wharncliffe True Crime, Wharncliffe Transport, Pen & Sword Select,
Pen & Sword Military Classics, Leo Cooper, The Praetorian Press,
Remember When, Seaforth Publishing and Frontline Publishing.

For a complete list of Pen & Sword titles please contact
PEN & SWORD BOOKS LIMITED
47 Church Street, Barnsley, South Yorkshire, S70 2AS, England
E-mail: enquiries@pen-and-sword.co.uk
Website: www.pen-and-sword.co.uk

Contents

Introduction

Throughout my career in flying I was continually being asked what the job was really like. Was it boring? Had I ever seen any flying saucers? Had I ever had any near misses? There was never enough time to give a complete answer. Over the years I evolved a couple of tongue-in-cheek throw-away lines, such as 'Well it's better than working' or 'It's just four over-stretched blokes up the front and seven over-excited girls down the back'.

It seemed that flying a big jet around the world was the second career choice of practically every red-blooded male I ever met, so the intent of this account is to provide a collage of a life in flying during a particular period of its evolution. It includes the nearest near miss of all time and, yes, a brush with something logically inexplicable.

A well-worn cliché is that airline flying comprises hours and hours of boredom punctuated by moments of sheer terror. This comment is more glib than correct on today's flight deck. While the cockpit procedures are routine, the hours aren't. Airline flying is a 24/7 life. Sundays and bank holidays are no different from Tuesdays and Thursdays, and 1.30 a.m. to 3.15 p.m. is as likely a day's work as 9 to 5.

While the rest of the world was going to work, I was usually going home to bed after an overnight flight from LA or somewhere allegedly exotic.

Flying is also an upside down life. Everything that's easy for the man in the street becomes difficult for a pilot; such as regular hours and a regular home life. I usually missed the school nativity play, wasted scores of theatre tickets and hundreds of pounds on unfinished night school courses. It isn't a subject on which I wish to elaborate, but it illustrates my point that it wasn't until after I retired at fifty-six that it dawned on me that most people routinely perform their ablutions sometime after breakfast.

On the plus side, and this is a huge plus, everything that is difficult for the man in the street, the best seat in the aeroplane, free worldwide travel, five-star hotels, cash allowances for food (sometimes confused in the wallet with beer money), sexy women in uniform and temptation, are all on tap. A final oddity of airline life is that most people delight in travel almost as an instinct. I have a theory that travel gives you a sideways view of life and is maybe an explanation of why artists and writers have always had the compulsion to travel. I have always been full of new ideas and am convinced that this innovation is a by-product of the lateral perspective that comes from continual travel.

Dr Peter Chapman, British Caledonian's Medical Officer, categorized two kinds of pilots, those who found the job very difficult and those who found it very easy. His more famous bon mot confirmed there were two other kinds of pilots, those who had piles and those who were going to have piles.

I don't know, at this stage, how honest I am going to be with these recollections; honesty is a risky commodity. While I have my log books to accurately confirm dates and places, please excuse me if some of the technical data will have to rely on the best of my recollection. I can only guarantee that this is the truth, not necessarily the whole truth, but something like the truth, so help me God. Where I am uncertain of my facts I will add a question mark in brackets (?).

I was not a pioneer, or as we say in the business, one of those who began flying when Pontius was a pilot. My era spanned the transition between the years when your flight safety was only as good as your captain, to today, when your safety devolves from the strength of a highly developed system. Put another way, I spanned the transition when flying stopped being a man's work and became mainly automated. I have no qualms about flying as a passenger today because I know how safe the aircraft is and how strong the procedures and associated systems are. I consider myself lucky to have grown up with an industry that was breaking new ground daily, but it was hairy at times as we learned. Besides the evolution of the aviation industry itself, there was a personal development from gung-ho fighter pilot to one of those straight and level guys.

Flying today has become almost an exact science. There are few decisions to make that are not already spelled out in the *Operations Manual*. It wasn't always like that. For example, when I started flying there were recommended weather minima for landing aids, but nothing specific for individual airfields; you had to build up your own minima from experience of a particular airfield, the type of landing aids available, the weather, the aeroplane and yourself. All take-off performance was unclassified so, apart from overall WAT limits (Weight Altitude Temperature), the maximum take-off weight at a particular airport or runway, was a captain's discretion item. A good captain then was someone who got the job done; someone you didn't hear any rumours about; reputation was all.

Today's young co-pilot will be horrified to read some of this account. I trust he or she will be generous in their recollection that all those rock solid safety procedures they take for granted today, that are a credit to an industry that handles high risk so competently, had to be learned from the often terminal experience of their predecessors. But horrified

3

or not, if you fancy becoming an airline pilot these days, it is very unlikely you will be confronted with the sort of problems that came my way because today's system is so scientifically well organized. Notwithstanding, you should be the kind of person who could deal with the situations you are going to read about should they ever happen, because, even recently, two captains found themselves with the total failure of both engines. One had to land in the Hudson River and another managed to stretch his glide to pancake a landing a hundred yards short of the runway threshold at London/Heathrow.

But let's start at the beginning.

CHAPTER 1

The Navy

My father always wanted to go to sea and see the world but his father, who was a ship's steward and knew the truth, wouldn't let him go. To get close to ships he had to settle for becoming a Liverpool docker. He must have been pretty smart, because he rose rapidly up the hierarchy and, by the time he was twenty-two he was a wharfinger, in complete charge of loading and unloading ship's cargoes onto the dockside and storing them in the warehouses so they could be readily located and collected by the consignees or shippers. His success probably saved his life because his attempt to enlist in the First World War that killed most of his generation was rejected because his occupation was reserved; nobody else knew where all the stuff was. Such was the depth of his experience in ships and shipping that, in 1930, in the midst of a severe economic depression, he landed the plum job of Purchasing Agent for Standard Oil (Esso) in Rio de Janeiro; he was responsible for ensuring that everything an oil company needed, or might need in Brazil, was already to hand, or shipborne and on the way. In 1939, seeing what was about to happen, he came back to Liverpool to do his bit for King and country.

My father was a self-taught graduate with a huge belief in books and the quality education he didn't get – but he made sure I did. When I was thirteen, my cunning father took me to Bangor, North Wales, and pointed to a handsome three-masted wooden wall ship-of-the-line moored in the Menai Straits (a sister ship to HMS *Victory*) and asked 'How would you like to go to that school son? They wear Navy officers' uniforms.'

What kid wouldn't fall for a line like that? I was hooked.

After my two years training in HMS *Conway*, in April 1950 I signed apprentice with Royal Mail Lines, a shipping company that specialized in the West Indies and South America (where I was born). Dad's master plan for me was that my splendid white dress uniform would catch the eye of a rich ranchero's daughter and we would all live in luxury ever after.

I eventually realized I was fulfilling my father's ambitions rather than my own. However, the one-man mutiny and why I left the sea after two years, breaking my father's heart, is another story; a decision reinforced by the advice from all my superiors that I should get out of the Merchant Navy while I was still young enough.

What is relevant is that as soon as I was no longer in the Merchant Service the National Service Draft Board quickly caught up with me. The RAF weren't interested in ex-sailors, the Army offered me a job in the cook house, and the Navy offered me a pilot's course in the Fleet Air Arm; it was not the most difficult decision of my life.

I had chanced upon a unique window in National Service. The War Office decided they might need more pilots for the anti-communist wars in Korea and Malaya, so they set out to ensure they had a sufficient reserve. Out of the entire history of National Service, this flying opportunity was only available to a few hundred national servicemen, so I was exceptionally lucky.

While I was waiting I thought it would be useful to get some driving experience so I got a job driving a lorry in my Uncle Fred's scrap business.

Looking back on it now, driving Uncle Fred's scrap lorries was an almost ideal preparation for what was to come. Besides the training in getting the job done under difficulties with his old scrap lorries, he had three men working in the yard. They lived off Scotland Road, had been together in the army and had survived Tobruk. Men who have bayoneted their way into another day of life after a German Afrika Korps charge have an aura. I didn't know much, but I knew I was in the presence of proven men. Cliff was the gaffer and operated the crane. Ginger was dying of TB and his two mates were carrying him, always giving him the easy jobs. And there was Sammy. Sammy was the smallest of the three, but it didn't take an A level in sensitivity to get the message that nobody messed with Sammy. He had the same dignified presence of an unexploded bomb. One day I was throwing heavy lead ingots into a skip and one landed on Sammy who, unknown to me, was inside! I expected to be killed. He accepted my profound apology with good grace. 'You should always check, young fella,' he said, and for the rest of my life, I always did.

Surprisingly, Sammy couldn't drive and one day he and I were bringing some heavy drums of lead BT cable from West Derby. It was a drizzly day, the roads were treacherous and we were ridiculously overloaded as usual. Besides this, the fuel pump wasn't working so I had to pump the fuel into the carburettor by slapping my hand over the intake every ten seconds or so to cause a suction. We were struggling uphill on a cobbled street, which was extra slippery in the drizzle. We gradually slithered to a halt with the wheels spinning. We were going nowhere, so I let the lorry roll backwards downhill until it had mounted the pavement. The concrete paving slabs gave much better traction even in the wet, so with the extra grip on one side and slapping the carburettor intake for fuel, we scrambled up to the main road at the top. When we finally got settled on the East Lancs Road Sammy gave me his opinion.

'I didn't think we would make dat,' he said. 'Quick thinkin' young fellah. Yous'll do alright on dat pilots' course.'

I glowed with pride to have the approbation of such a man as this. But he taught me one far more valuable lesson on the same day. As we got closer to town he announced that we would go to his house for a cup of tea.

Frankly I was not keen, and not keen for all the very worst of snobby reasons, but nobody messed with Sammy, so we turned off Scotty Road, parked and went in.

Then I was ashamed. I was ashamed of myself because his little council two up two down was clean, neat and spotless. His wife was a delight, a sunny, cheerful credit to Liverpool womanhood and his kids, just home from school, were respectfully in awe to meet someone who was going to be a fighter pilot.

When we got back to the yard Cliff demanded to know what had taken us so long, so I explained about the weather, the weight of the lorry and going to Sammy's for tea.

Cliff and Ginger were gobsmacked! 'We've known Sammy all our lives and never been inside 'is 'ouse,' said Cliff. For me, the public schoolboy, a very large chunk of something less than creditable in myself was also bayoneted on that afternoon.

In due course, in December 1953 a travel voucher arrived to travel to RAF Hornchurch for aircrew selection assessment, comprising IQ intelligence, medical and physical co-ordination tests. The most testing of these was a TV monitor screen with a one-inch circle in the middle set in front of a control column similar to a pilot's joystick. When the test began, a dot appeared in the middle of the circle and began to wander all over the screen. The objective was to use the joystick to keep the dot inside the one-inch circle. It was not easy, but a very efficient way to separate the quick from the dead.

These tests must have been successful because next came a further voucher to Royal Naval Air Station (RNAS) Lee-on-Solent (HMS *Daedalus*) for further consideration by the Navy. This involved more searching IQ tests and practical group tests in the gym. My test involved getting my team over a twelve-foot gorge with only two eleven-foot planks for equipment; not particularly difficult if you have any comprehension of leverage. Only two of our group finished our tasks in the time allotted, and it was these two, and fifty others, who reported to HMS *Daedalus* for induction into the Navy as Naval Airmen, Second Class.

Uniform issue, bell-bottoms and some diabolical itchy underpants, was followed by the usual square bashing. 'Cream of Britain's youth is it?' our Chief Petty Officer sneered. 'Officers? We'll soon see about that.' Two weeks later we set sail in two aircraft carriers, HMS *Implacable* and *Indefatigable*, for exercises in Gibraltar and the Mediterranean. There is something quite momentous about a carrier going to sea – a carrier is more than a ship, it is a mobile city.

Although it was surreptitious, we were all very carefully watched and assessed for OLQs (officer like qualities) in the Navy's unique Nelsonian way. Having had wardroom status, I found life in bell-bottoms claustrophobic and a bit of a strain, but at least I was familiar with sleeping in a hammock. I kept a tight lid on my feelings because the end objective was such a desirable readymade career opportunity.

A couple of our intake failed this hurdle and one was back-classed to try again. The survivors, now known as 37 RNVR Pilots' Course, were introduced to Gieves & Hawkes to be measured for officers' uniforms then sent away for leave before reporting to Gosport (HMS *Siskin*) for pre-flight training.

The lifestyle contrast between communal naval airman, second class, queuing up for meals in the canteen, and mid-shipman in the gunroom, where meals were served to you, where you slept in your own room, where you signed chits for your drinks and paid for them at the end of the month when your Mess bill arrived, was spectacularly uplifting.

We lapped up the privilege and began to feel like the alleged cream of Britain's youth.

Pre-flight training consisted of lectures in theory of flight, pilot navigation, engines, engine handling and meteorology. We learned that an aircraft flies by means of lift produced by the wings, and that the sole function of the engine was to provide the forwards motion that produced an airflow over the wings, which are set at a slight angle to the flow so as to produce a suction (lift) on top of the wing and a pressure on the underside. The physics of this may seem debatable to a sceptic, but thousands of times, every day, a 200mph airflow lifts several hundred tons of jumbo into the sky in a safe and almost precisely controllable manner.

We were shown many instructional movies on survival in the jungle, the desert and at sea in a rubber dinghy. There was one thought-provoking graphical description of Einstein's theory of relativity to reassure us that we needed to get a lot closer to light speed than Mach 1 (the speed of sound) before we were in any danger of disappearing into Einstein's warp one hyperspace.

The induction into the Navy continued, with weapon training (pistols, rifles, Bren guns and clay pigeon) and I used to hang about the airfield and cadge flights in anything that had a spare seat. There was a memorable day trip in a submarine. The commander of the submarine told me he shuddered at the mere thought of leaving the ground in an aircraft whereas I shuddered as I descended the ladder into the bowels of his sub, but for a very different reason; more about this incident will follow. Seagoing officers in the Navy are known affectionately as fish-heads whereas aviators are known dismissively as pin-heads.

During this period we had our first fatality when George Elworthy was killed in a car crash. I had a near miss during clay pigeon shooting. I was waiting my turn with my shot-gun under my arm when one of the course leaned in and said 'I bet that gun isn't loaded', and he pulled the trigger. A largish hole appeared in the ground alongside my right foot.

We may have fancied ourselves as the cream of Britain's youth, but we were very young and inexperienced.

After a final exam there were a couple more failures and the remainder were posted to RAF Syerston for flying training.

The 'Wings' course was nine months long, comprising three months on the Prentice, a fixed undercarriage trainer, and six months on the Harvard. My instructor was Master Pilot Isaacs who sent me off solo after six hours; I do think having driven cars and lorries was a help. One piece of his advice that I followed religiously was always to wear a pair of stout shoes because, in flying, you never knew when you might have to walk the last few hundred miles. We were superbly instructed in every aspect of flying, such as circuits and landings, recovery from stalling and spinning, aerobatics, navigational exercises all over Britain, night flying and flying solely by instruments. There was even an escape and evasion exercise where we were dropped off from a lorry at night somewhere in the country. We had a map, but we didn't know where we were on it; this was to simulate parachuting down into enemy territory. The objective was to get back into our home airfield by any means available over a weekend with the police and local Home Guard units out hunting for us. I was captured and given a sufficiently unpleasant interrogation for me to make up my mind that I wasn't ever going to get caught so easily again.

There is little to mention about flying training except to say I absolutely loved every minute; the feeling of freedom, freedom to go north or south, left or right and even up or down! The only thing I hated was the morning gym.

I have long held the opinion that the heart is an elastic muscle with a certain inherited number of cycles leading to an inevitable fatigue failure. I saw little point in wasting any precious heart beats on pointless exercise and no advantage in a daily demonstration that my toes were in the same place they were yesterday. I base this controversial theory on the observation that sports stars do not seem to live longer than sloth stars; if somebody had noticed to the contrary it would be common knowledge by now. Instead, we see world champion boxers shuffling about with obvious signs of physical misuse, footballers in wheelchairs with ruined knees, golfers, ballet dancers and tennis stars who keep hip replacement surgeons in their Mercedes lifestyle. I maintain the only exercise worthy of an officer and a gentleman is press ups, and even then, only when a lady is involved.

These pointless contortions were performed in the parking area outside the front door of the Mess. This front door was in the base of the U-shaped Mess building. My room on the first floor overlooked this area, so, for morning gym and roll call, I used to call out 'present' from the warmth and comfort of my bedroom window. This arrangement seemed agreeable to all involved since I was never involved in any negative feedback.

There was a steady chop rate, which gradually reduced our numbers from forty-eight down to twenty-four. A trainee from another course, Curas-Thompson, killed himself in a Harvard having taken a bet that he could pull through from a thousand feet (pull through: the second half of a loop, starting from upside down). He might have won his bet except he neglected to allow for the fact that the ground where he started from was already three hundred feet high; the remaining seven hundred feet proved insufficient and he made a large black hole in a cornfield. His misfortune was an object lesson to us all that, in flying, you were on your own and that you needed to be pretty sharp about it.

Nine months later I got my Wings. Admiral Sherbrooke VC flew into Syerston to pin the badge on my sleeve. I was proud of myself. I was no longer under instruction; I was a fully qualified Fleet Air Arm pilot.

My girlfriend came to see the ceremony and afterwards I took her into the control tower. A Harvard was on the approach. Watch this, I said. This is how it's done.

Unfortunately, the Harvard pilot must have landed with his brakes on because, as soon as his wheels touched the ground, he went base over apex in a perfect somersault and ended upside down on the runway. The air traffic controller hit the alarm and the fire engine dashed over. Luckily for the Harvard he didn't catch fire. The controller said he was always surprised by how stately and ponderous flying was when everything was going well, and how quickly a situation could turn into a runaway nightmare, with aircraft careering all over the airfield.

At some point we had already been assessed as either more suitable as fighter pilots or anti-submarine pilots. I guess it was a student's natural temperament and proficiency in aerobatics that dictated this selection; the steady types went to anti-sub and the gung-ho went to fighters.

As a National Service midshipman selected for fighter training, I had a couple of options. The Navy was gambling that we would all sign on for a four or eight-year short service commission, which would involve a posting to RNAS Lossiemouth for a jet conversion on to Sea Hawks. Those who declined would go to RNVR squadrons and become weekend reserve pilots. The inventory for 764 Squadron, RNVR Fighter School, HMS *Heron*, Yeovilton, was the Seafire XVII (the Spitfire with an arrester hook).

The Spitfire, without doubt, is the most elegant and beautiful construction ever manufactured by mankind and the Seafire XVII, elegantly slim with a bubble canopy, is the prettiest of all the marks. Every pilot I've ever met has moaned with envy and never queried my choice. So, from the Harvard – maximum speed 110 knots – the next step was the Seafire with a maximum speed of 480 knots. I couldn't wait. My plan was to celebrate my first solo over a pint in the gunroom and casually mention that it was very nice to see 480 knots on the clock; never, never ever underestimate overconfidence.

The Pilot's Notes were informative, with some novel cautionary hints for a Harvard pilot; such as the Griffon 47 (which succeeded the famous Merlin) was such a powerful engine it would overheat unless airflow cooled within a few minutes of start up. A second tip was that, in the pre-flight vital actions, pilots were recommended to tighten the throttle friction nut and then tighten it again extra hard. Another was that inverted flight should be logged in the A700 (the individual aircraft's maintenance and serviceability record) because of the possibility of dumping glycol during upside down negative G. Most interesting was the warning that, at 430 knots, the Seafire XVII could experience trim reversal. I'd seen David Lean's film *Sound Barrier*, so I knew all I needed to know about control reversal; you just had to be sanguine about your instinctive reactions and move the stick in the opposite direction. Cool!

At around this time we learned that one of our number on the anti-submarine course, Mike Eason(?) had dived into the Bristol Channel. Apparently, weak on aerobatics, he was only able to barrel roll to the right. When following his instructor in a 'chase me Charlie', his instructor rolled to the left; Eason got half way and lost it. Attempting to pull through to recover he had found himself, like Curas-Thompson, with insufficient height to succeed.

So the great day arrived and we were duly authorized for Seafire solo familiarization to include stall practice and recovery. The squadron didn't have a two-seat trainer, so, apart from some familiarization in a two-seat Firefly, we were in at the deep end. I was more than up for it. Get airborne as quickly as possible to avoid overheating the Griffon. That curious note about the throttle friction nut, what was all that about?

The Fighter School's first solo day was a great event at Yeovilton. The regular Navy Seahawk jet squadrons all took the day off, camping out on the control tower roof with binoculars and crates of beer to watch the fun. They knew what was coming; Christians were being thrown to the lions.

We, the *innocenti*, started engines and taxied out, having to tack from side to side of the perimeter track so we could see what was in front of the huge, throaty, Griffon – such an orgasmic sound. At the threshold we swung into wind, did a quick run-up and pre-flight vital actions. To a man, we did up the throttle friction nut as tight as seem necessary on the day.

Our instructor's brief was to:

> ... apply full left rudder with the power even before you let go the brakes because there will be an immediate right swing due to the narrow undercarriage and the reduced rudder area [the Seafire's already small rudder was further reduced to accommodate the deck landing arrester hook]. Whatever you do, don't brake it straight, hold full rudder and wait for the increasing airflow to make the rudder effective.

Double cool!

After the Harvard, the hit as you let go of the brakes in a Seafire was like being slammed in the back by a lorryload of lead in a motorway pile up. Tail up – airborne – control column in the right hand, throttle lever in the left as usual.

In the Spitfire, the undercarriage lever is on the right hand side of the panel – you have to swap hands. You move your left hand to the control column to free the right hand to reach over to select undercarriage up. The trouble was that as soon as you let go of the throttle, the fierce acceleration caused the throttle to snap closed – because the throttle friction nut was not done up tight enough! This was what those bastards had come to see. As each Seafire got airborne it lost power and staggered like a freshly shot pheasant. Each take-off then became a roller coaster ride. The jet jockeys in the goofers were falling about with delight. (Goofers is Navy slang for a safe place from which observers with a taste for *Schadenfreude* could watch deck landings.)

Doooown she goes. Uuuuup she comes. Doooown she goes again. On their first solo in Seafires, most pilots are passing 3,000 feet before they sort out how to get the wheels up, which is deliciously amusing to other pilots who've been through it; and there were the first attempts at landings still to come!

Having a Spitfire strapped to your backside is the second most exhilarating experience in human life. The Navy didn't pay me enough money to afford a bicycle, but at least they'd loaned me a Seafire to play with. Never mind the familiarization detail as briefed, I had my own agenda.

I climbed up to 13,000 feet, an all-day job for a Harvard, but surprisingly quick in a Seafire. I looked down at the lovely Somerset countryside, picked out a huge golden cornfield as an aiming point and winged over into a steep dive.

At full throttle the speed built up quickly: 200 knots, 300 knots, 400. This was real flying!

Then I noticed something peculiar. My right wing was dropping but I was already holding full left aileron! I realized my problem immediately, control reversal, as described in the Pilot's Notes. Confidently, I applied full right aileron and was somewhat disconcerted when the Spitfire obligingly flipped on to its back.

There is nothing inherently dangerous about flying upside down, or in being in a steep dive, or doing something in the region of 480 knots and getting quite close to the ground, or even of not being too sure what your ailerons might do next. However, put all these factors together and a different conclusion quickly emerges. I was well down the pan-pan-pan (pan screamed three times is the recognized international radio distress call from a pilot in urgent need of assistance).

The classic recovery from being inverted is to pull through, and I almost tried that, even though I knew I didn't have nearly enough height to succeed – but I do recall thinking this would make a much bigger hole than Curas-Thompson.

Suddenly wise beyond my 180 hours, 4½ minutes, I elected to bunt out (a bunt: an unpleasant, rarely performed eyeball-popping manoeuvre like a loop, but performed upside down – or inside out if you prefer). I pushed hard on the control column and immediately wished I'd also tightened my harness along with the throttle friction nut. I came right out of the seat and the negative G pinned me into the bubble canopy. I was having difficulty continuing with my unusual attitude recovery because I could barely reach the control column and was reduced to pushing the pole with the tip of my finger. This was clearly likely to end unhappily until I realized I could do better with my foot, so I gave the stick a hefty heave with my boot.

I was both surprised and relieved to see a crack of blue and the horizon reappeared going relatively upwards. I pushed with my foot until the view was completely blue. I yanked the aileron fully over. I wasn't sure which way it would roll, I would sort that out later, but she rolled out normally.

For the technically minded I figured out later what had happened. The Seafire XVII is just a huge engine with wings. In a dive, as the speed increases the propeller wash on the rudder also increases and to keep the aircraft in trim (i.e. keep the top needle centred), you have to apply increasing right rudder in balance. Above 430 knots (if I recall the figure correctly), the aeroplane suddenly leaves the propeller wash behind. If you don't notice this transition you are left with a boot full of right rudder you no longer need and obligingly the aircraft will begin a roll to the right. A ham fist of right aileron was not the ideal solution.

As I rolled out and fell back into the seat I recalled that I still had to land this handful of extreme engineering that had nearly killed me yet whose magical stability had flown me out of trouble in the following split second.

In subdued mood I reverted to the detail as briefed. I practised every conceivable kind of stall and recovery, only going back for my first attempt at landing when the fuel began to get desperately low. I did a textbook approach and a nice three-point landing, but as soon as we touched the ground she went into a vicious right swing. The rudder was very stiff and the Spitfire's incipient ground loop was developing nicely when I heard the instructor's voice in my ear (from the caravan) saying 'Power on, 108, power on.' This advice worked okay, except I over-cooked it and found myself threatening to get airborne again – heading straight for the control tower. I was told afterwards that the jet jockeys on the tower roof abandoned their beer and were baling-out down the backstairs: good.

The voice in my ear called 'Cut your throttle 108. Cut your throttle. Since this voice got me out of trouble the last time, I obeyed, even though there was another landing still to come. Braking became a desperate attempt to avoid tenders for a new air traffic control tower.

I only just made it. There was such a pile of grass under my wheels I couldn't taxi and as the Griffon was threatening to overheat I had to cut the engine. Embarrassingly, I was pushed back to dispersal by two disgusted pilot's mates who absolutely loathed their lovely engineering masterpieces being bent and twisted by the most inexperienced pilot's in the Navy. For the whole of that summer there was this humiliating curved scar of scorched grass leading from the runway, across the airfield and ending up in two miniature haystacks a few yards short of Commander Air's office window.

I was honest enough in the A700. I mentioned that the rudder seemed a bit stiff and that I had flipped upside down in one of the stalls, so the glycol tank should be checked for negative G spillage.

When I went to my locker to park my flying overall I noticed I had an ugly wheal across each shoulder from where the seat harness and the negative G had dug in and stopped me from going clean through the bubble canopy.

My pilot's mate came back and said he wasn't surprised I had a stiff rudder because there was compacted wheat in the counterbalance of the fin hinge. 'It wasn't there when I did the pre-flight,' he said belligerently, 'how had that got there?' I went a bit pale. I knew I must have been low, but not that low! My desperate lunge at the control column with my foot must have flicked my tail through the tops of a wheat field upside down at 480 knots! And I wasn't even sitting in the seat but was lying in the bubble canopy like a foetus! I put out a hand to stop the locker from falling over.

'There was a lot of straw being blown about in the run-up area,' I extemporized. 'I must have sucked some up and it got jammed in by the airflow.'

'Jammed?' he echoed. 'It was jammed all right. I had to gouge it out with a hammer and screwdriver'.

However, I still had one more urgent problem to deal with that day. Somehow, I had to walk the mile back to the wardroom without a change of underpants.

As I shimmied back to the Mess I was an emotional and physical wreck and reasoned I was obviously not suited to a pilot's life and I made up my mind to resign. At the Mess, after a shower, for peace and quiet I went into the TV room to write my resignation. I turned on the radio and found some classical music to scare intruders away. The BBC were playing Vaughan Williams' *Rhapsody on a Theme by Thomas Tallis*, and as this lovely music washed over me and soaked in I became fatalistic. So what if I did kill myself, the world didn't need me to keep on turning. So I decided not to go LMF (lack of moral fibre), tore up the letter and resigned myself to my fate.

I think I managed to avoid the telltale eye twitch of the overstretched pilot and slowly I got my confidence back.

Fighter School provided several choice moments that were good for the soul; such as a squadron formation climb up to 30,000 feet making our first contrails; a low level navigation exercise alone over the sea, utterly dependent on the engine and compass for survival. The best was joining the circuit, Navy style, at 300 feet flat out, cutting the throttle and hearing the huge Griffon back-firing, spluttering and complaining like cannon fire all the way downwind and, if you had judged it right, not touching the throttle again until after the landing. By the end of that marvellous summer, swanning around the south coast pretending to be a Battle of Britain pilot, I was as insufferable as before.

My log book shows that I flew fifty hours and fifty minutes in Spitfires; most of that was upside down avoiding attempts by my course mates to get on my tail. The game was to sneak up behind someone, line them up in the gunsight and call 'Rat ... atat ... tat' over the radio, and then celebrate this victory with a beer paid for by the careless victim in the gunroom bar.

This was a magical time so poignantly set to words by Spitfire Pilot Officer Magee in his searing poem 'High Flight'.

> Oh I have slipped the surly bonds of earth
> And danced the skies on laughter silvered wings;
> Sunward I've climbed and joined the tumbling mirth
> Of sun-split clouds – and done a hundred things
> You've not dreamed of; wheeled and soared and swung
> High in the sun-lit silence. Hovering there
> I've chased the shouting wind along, and flung
> My eager craft through footless halls of air;
> Up, up the long delirious, burning blue
> I've topped the wind-swept heights with easy grace
> Where never lark nor even eagle flew;
> And while, with silent lifting mind I've trod
> The high untrespassed sanctity of space,
> Put out my hand and touched the face of God.

(Reproduced by kind permission of
This England Publishing)

Every pilot knows that feeling, which underpins the brotherhood of all aviators.

Seafire 108 is still available to see at the Fleet Air Arm Museum, RNAS Yeovilton. Should you happen to visit, give her a hug from me. The only negative aspect of 764 Squadron's Fighter School is that, once you've flown a Spitfire, you can only feel so very very sorry for sports cars.

At the end of the course I thought long and hard about 'signing on' for a four or eight-year short service commission in the Royal Navy proper. The end cash bonus was designed to be attractive (enough to buy a new car), and I was tempted. That I didn't sign on was probably due to an experience in Brazil when I was in the Merchant Navy.

We were anchored in Rio de Janeiro harbour. As the sun rose and illuminated that most marvellous of cities, aeroplanes began to take off from the nearby Santos Dumont airport.

These aircraft had to make an immediate tight turn to stay over the water and inside the harbour to avoid the surrounding mountains that were still shrouded in low cloud and morning mist. I decided on the spot that I wanted a job like that; a job where you did a bit more than clean the bloody brass work and spend those precious few days in harbour on cargo watch, six hours on and six hours off, trying to stop the dockers from plundering the bonded store whisky. There was never any time to go ashore further than the nearest bar, but, most unsatisfactory of all, there were no women on cargo boats. When the ship got back to London I wrote to BOAC (British Overseas Airways Corporation) and offered my services. BOAC politely replied that I should apply again when I had a pilot's licence. I didn't sign on for a short service commission because I decided to get a Commercial Pilot's Licence. I had this great compulsion to handle complicated machinery, see the world and meet women; civil flying promised all three.

After Fighter School we were posted to our RNVR squadrons. Because I lived near Liverpool I was posted to 1831 Squadron based at RNAS Stretton near Warrington in Lancashire. 1831 Squadron was equipped with the Hawker Sea Fury.

21

The Sea Fury is the world's fastest single-engine piston fighter. It had an extremely powerful Centaurus radial engine with a huge five-bladed propeller. She was a delight to fly and virtually viceless. Her only vice was that, when flying at low speeds, if you slammed open the throttle, instead of the propeller rotation increasing, the aeroplane would rotate around the propeller. This feature was graphically demonstrated when one of our squadron realized that he was about to land on the perimeter track, which, in the snow, he had mistaken for the runway. From a low and slow configuration he applied full power to go round again. Instead, the Fury flipped upside down. He recovered from this and found himself in danger of flying through an adjacent hangar. So he applied full power to escape and flipped upside down again. From this unhappy position he clipped the hangar roof, slid over the top upside down and fell into a pile of coke on the far side. The Navy lands with an open cockpit hood, and he came to rest across a barb wire fence about two inches before his scalp. It was not his time.

Sadly, his time came a few weeks later when he disappeared over the Irish Sea on a flight to Eglinton together with his Flight Leader, Johnny Hamer. It is pure speculation, but the weather was foul, and in such conditions a pair might have adopted a 'snake climb' procedure. This involved the number two latching on to the leader's tail in the fog of cloud. The trick was not to lose contact with your leader because, if you attempted a blind catch up, it was very likely that you would misjudge it and accelerate through the tail of the aircraft ahead before you could stop. The huge Centaurus propeller would have had no problem slicing off the leader's tail.

Besides this unlucky duo, we began to hear about the fate of other colleagues from the 37 RNVR course who had signed on for short service commissions. My roommate at Gosport, Steve Carter, was killed in a collision with an RAF Vampire in the circuit at RNAS Ford. Jim King suffered vertigo while night flying and dived into the ground. In

Hong Kong, Roger Lowson had flown into a stuffed cloud (a cloud with a mountain inside), Daisy Flower hit the ground short of the runway and exploded while doing a GCA (a ground controlled approach by radar), probably because of a miss-set or faulty altimeter and the pint-loving John Grant died from a heart attack, possibly from seeing his Mess bill.

The Navy decided to postpone our carrier deck-landing training because of the experience of 35 RNVR course. A fully worked-up aircraft carrier would average about 3,000 deck landings per incident, a training carrier would expect to average about 1,500. At one time 35 RNVR course had a tally of three incidents for one landing. It was decided that the necessary techniques for successful deck landings in a Sea Fury were beyond the grasp of the newly graduated pilot.

There is a deal of truth in this. The Fury is a pussy cat to land doing a wheeler (landing with the tail off the ground), but the problem was that doing a wheeler on the carrier would cause the hook to miss all the arrester wires. So you had to do a three-pointer where the main and tailwheels all touch the ground at the same time. The problem with three-pointers in a Fury was that, because of the huge engine, you couldn't see ahead, so you were landing on a ship that you couldn't see, having to judge your height and level attitude by looking rapidly from side to side. Phew!

Since the margin of error for a carrier landing is non-existent, getting the aircraft in the right place at the right speed becomes the responsibility of the batsman.

Batsmen were a unique class of characters. On every carrier each landing was registered for later debriefing and criticism in the unique batsman's shorthand, logged usually by a trainee pilot. The batsman might call out 'BALLS', which decoded as Began Approach Low, Landed Slow. The most dreaded comment decoded as Cannot Understand New Technique!

The technique designed to cope with all the Sea Fury's peculiarities was a normal Navy circuit at 300 feet with a continuous turn aiming to line up with the carrier's flight deck with only a few hundred feet to go. As you got to that point you could no longer see the ship behind the engine and would be in the hands of 'Bats'. Bats would indicate the final adjustments you needed to make in order to stay alive and, if and when he was happy, he would signal 'cut'. On receipt of the 'cut' the pilot had to cut the throttle and, uniquely and contrary to automatic reflexes, you had to allow the nose to drop. This would give you a quick last look at reality to level the wings and align your motion with the flight deck centre line. Then you had to jerk the stick back into your guts and pancake onto the deck in the three-point attitude. The sangfroid required to perform this technique was traumatic even for experienced pilots.

Otherwise the Fury was a delight to fly. Two trips stand out in my memory. One was a visit to my old school, HMS *Conway*, where I did a couple of low passes that were probably a little too enthusiastic and caused a detail on the parade ground to dive for cover. My belated apologies are tendered. Another was a legal low-level exercise to the Firth of Forth to rendezvous with a cruiser that needed to calibrate its radar. It was a gin clear day, and I flew at a low level out of the Mersey, up the coast of the Irish Sea, marvelling in its beauty, a minor diversion to see Fingal's Cave, then flew low level along the Caledonian Canal and Loch Ness, keeping a sharp eye open for monsters. Finally, I flew into the Moray Firth and southwards around the coast back to Edinburgh and the Firth of Forth to find my cruiser.

The RNVR was the perfect complement for my civil flying ambitions. A weekend pilot was allowed to do three days' 'continuous' at any time, so, as long as I kept within that, I was on full pay, but in three-day spurts. This allowed me to get on with (pay for) the various tests required for a Commercial Pilot's Licence.

I was beginning to get the hang of the Navy. I discovered that I could telephone various squadron commanders and ask if I could join them for some experience. They were all most willing to oblige, and in this way I got myself a twin-engine rating at Rochester, an instrument flying course and a detachment to 781 Squadron (the Navy's mini airline), which gave me a Rapide rating for my civil licence and a Dove course at de Havillands of Hatfield, as well as some useful Dove handling experience. I used to assign myself to all these useful qualifications. What is remarkable about the Navy is that I noticed all my covert manoeuvres had been registered by the Admiralty, and three months later in the CW lists (postings and promotions orders) I would read Midshipman R G Williams – to RNAS Rochester for twin conversion training, accurately dated three months previously. Should the reader be in any doubt, I can assure you the Royal Navy is a spectacularly efficient organization at any level you can think of. With the exception of Horatio Nelson, inevitably the Navy changes you more than you change it and marks you for life. Throughout my career I could always spot a Navy pilot from the cut of his jib.

The next stage in qualifying for my Commercial Pilot's Licence involved examinations in air law, navigation, flight planning, flight instruments, radio aids and meteorology with the Civil Aviation Authority (CAA) in London's Berkeley Square, where I could lodge very cheaply at the nearby RNVR Club. Next came engineering exams by the Air Registration Board in aircraft construction and systems. A pilot has to prove he has a thorough technical knowledge of any aircraft he proposes to put on his licence together with specific actual flying experience. For a Group 2 (co-pilot's) rating a pilot has to have performed six take-offs and landings. For a Group 1 (captain's) rating, the requirements were extended to cover such things as night and strong crosswind landings. These flying requirements were usually funded by the company you work for, but if you were not yet employed, you had to pay yourself, which could be a very expensive option, so usually ab initios picked on something cheap and simple like the Chipmunk or Tiger Moth to get the licence – which got you a job.

The trickiest of these tests was the dreaded Instrument Rating, which involved a flight test in a de Havilland Dove with a Ministry Inspector. What was difficult about the Instrument Rating (besides the cost) was that it was a completely different sort of flying than I was used to, requiring a pilot to maintain a precise course, height and airspeed foreign to the nature of the gung-ho fighter pilot.

The next stage of my time in the RN was the squadron's re-equipment with the Supermarine Attacker, the only jet with a tailwheel (considered at the time as a necessity for deck landings). The Attacker provided me with more narrow shaves in two years than the whole of the rest of my career.

Before we were let loose in the Attacker we had to do a jet conversion course, which was entrusted to Airwork, a civil contractor. This involved two weeks flying the Meteor 7 at St David's airfield in South Wales.

However, there were a couple of things we had to do before being let loose on a jet. One was to experience being fired out of a cockpit from an ejector seat. This is just like being fired out from a fairground cannon. The ejector seat was set in a thirty foot high ramp, and when you pulled the blind over your face the seat fired off, just like the aeroplane. You would suddenly find yourself thirty foot higher than you were a split second ago and, it was rumoured, a centimetre shorter from compressed spinal discs! The function of the blind over the face was to avoid the considerable readjustment of your facial features that a 400mph airflow could cause.

The other requirement was an oxygen awareness course, which involved going into a large air tight tank, about the size of a ship's boiler, from which the air could be extracted to simulate high altitude. Each candidate was connected to an oxygen system and mask, just like in an aeroplane. At a simulated thirty thousand feet, each candidate in turn would have his oxygen turned off to demonstrate the dangers of anoxia.

The danger of anoxia is the victim's complete lack of awareness of the onset of oxygen starvation, which leads to unconsciousness within a few minutes. There are a few telltale signs, such as slurred speech and irrational behaviour, which might only be noticed by an alert third party such as a wingman or air traffic controller. There comes a moment just before complete unconsciousness when a victim becomes susceptible to clear and concise commands. Each pilot was given a simple task to do as the anoxia began – such as to deal a hand of solitaire. Judging the moment, the instructor would order the student to take off his shoes and the student would obey. The oxygen was then restored and the student would recover and continue with the allotted task as if nothing had happened. The instructor would ask him how he felt, and the student might reply that he felt fine, under the impression he must be superhumanly impervious to anoxia. Then the instructor would ask him 'Who took off your shoes?' The dumbfounded student would have no recollection whatsoever. The lasting value of the demonstration was in observing the lethal effects of anoxia on others, which, in a very practical way, demonstrated the mortal danger of forgetting to open your oxygen valve in your pre-take-off vital actions.

All the instructors at Airwork, St David's, were extremely experienced ex-RAF or Navy trainers and I met some great characters; such as Paddy Prior, an English Irishman, who I was to meet again at British Caledonian Airways (BCAL) and 'Dinger' Bell.

In all my years of flying, Paddy Prior was the only one ever to claim to have seen a flying saucer and Dinger Bell was probably the most superb outright handler of an aeroplane that I ever came across. At the end of a detail Dinger would ask if I minded if he took over for a bit of practice, and I sat in wonder as he closed the thrust lever and aerobatted all the way to circuit downwind with loops, rolls and stall turns. It was humbling to watch. Except for stall turns, where it was not possible, the top needle would be glued in the centre of the turn and slip meter, something hard to achieve, particularly upside down at the top of a loop. The stall turn is a curious manoeuvre, a freak of aeronautics where the aircraft is pulled up to the vertically upwards, then as the speed decays, just before the aircraft would normally fall out of the sky, full rudder is applied and the aircraft gracefully wings over from vertically upwards to vertically downwards with nothing on the airspeed indicator except the maker's name. My instructor claimed that a stall turn is the only manoeuvre that an aeroplane can do that a bird cannot.

Godfrey Place, VC was also on the course. He remained modestly reticent about his wartime experiences in midget submarines no matter how much Scotch we attempted to pour down his throat.

Flying jets was mainly a problem of getting used to the higher speeds where events happened much more quickly from jet engines that delivered more power, but delivered it much more slowly. For example, on one detail, I was doing circuits and landings. Because of the speed of events, I got out of sequence with the aircraft and made an approach with the wheels selected up rather than down. An alert air traffic control officer saved me from this supreme embarrassment and fired off a red Very flare, which warned me to go round again. The Very also alerted the whole station to my embarrassment, which cost me a lot of beer that evening. On one detail I climbed up to 40,000 feet in the unpressurized Meteor but, feeling lumpy, thought it wise not to stay long. St David's was another magical time, nearly as splendid as the Seafire summer.

For such a handsome aircraft, the Attacker's design was not a success because the aircraft could either fly well and have fifty minutes of endurance, or fly like a pregnant whale for 120 minutes with a 200-gallon(?) belly tank slung underneath.

The Pilot's Notes read like an obituary. It had warnings such as, 'if the fire warning light comes on, do not attempt to extinguish, eject immediately', and another was 'as Mach increases the nose gets progressively heavy. At above .83 Mach the nose may become too heavy to hold leading to loss of control' (and probable structural failure – although the Notes only implied such). The Attacker also had a history of catastrophic engine failures and airborne explosions, which one of my close shaves was able to throw some light on.

We were practising a formation take-off. Pete Barlow was leading and I was number two on the left. The worst job on a formation take-off is the number four who has to line up behind the leader, slightly to one side to avoid ingesting his leader's hot exhaust gases. On reaching flying speed, the number four has to hold his plane down on the runway until the leader has lifted off in front of him so that the lift from his own wings is not ruined by the leader's downwash. Number four has to trust his leader to get off the ground early enough to leave him enough runway to get clean air for his own lift off. There is little margin for error on a formation take-off.

Because there was a two-second delay before you started to move after brakes release and we obviously all needed to start to move at the same moment, Pete called 'Brakes' and all four of us let go the brakes simultaneously. During the roll I suddenly noticed that Pete's ground/flight socket cover, a saucer sized aluminium plate that covered the ground/flight electrics socket in flight, was not housed correctly and was flapping about, dangling from a flimsy bit of lavatory chain. This flimsy chain was not going to hold the cover once the speed had built up to several hundred knots. What worried me was that it was exactly in line with his engine intake. When the chain parted the plate would be sucked into the intake and cause all kinds of havoc to the compressor blades, which were spinning at roughly 12,000 times per minute. These red hot blades would become detached and cause havoc in the engine compartment. If one of these pierced the fuel tank, an explosion was very likely. My problem was how to stop a formation take-off safely and I had zero seconds to think about it before we were committed to a take-off. I called 'Blue Leader, your ground/flight socket cover is dangling loose. Blue Flight abandon take-off. Close your throttles NOW.' Thankfully, all four of us complied and we rolled to a formation stop with about fifty yards of concrete to spare. I realized that we had stumbled across a possible explanation for the Attacker's record of unexplained engine fires and explosions that the Pilot's Notes recommended should be treated with an immediate eject.

I had a lot of interesting experiences with the Attacker. Perhaps the most interesting to pilots was the occasion when I unwisely attempted a stall turn at 20,000 feet with an almost full belly tank. I fell immediately into a spin. This was a most unique spin and not anything like as described in any Pilot's Notes. The aircraft was falling like it had just been dumped off a lorry and rotating quite fast, roughly twenty RPM in the roll axis. At the same time I was yawing slowly and horizontally around the horizon. I immediately initiated the standard spin recovery: opposite rudder, pause, then push the stick forwards. Nothing happened. I waited a moment and tried the drill once again. Nothing happened. I tried a third time again without success. So I thought, this is it, you are going to have to eject. I reached up to pull the ejector seat blind over my face when I thought I would have one last try, but I would do everything in the opposite sense. I applied same direction rudder, paused and pulled the stick back. She slipped out of the spin like an Olympic champion high board diver's entry into the pool.

On another occasion I was asked to do a flight check on an Attacker fresh out of major overhaul. I was asked to check everything because the aircraft had been completely dismantled and rebuilt. I took off, checked all the systems, threw her about a bit and everything seemed normal. I was just about to go home when I considered whether to check the stall speeds. After my inverted spin experience when I nearly banged out, I was nervous of the Attacker's stall recovery. I forget the actual figures, but clean, I was expecting a stall at around 105 knots. At 120 knots she suddenly flipped onto her back. I checked the flaps, extended stall speed and this was also 15 knots higher than it should be. I thanked my lucky stars for deciding to check the stall speeds because to flip upside down on finals would have been embarrassing and probably fatal, so I made my approach with a corrected stall safe speed. I thought the problem must be an airspeed indicator error caused by a misaligned pitot tube, but a red-faced engineer lieutenant told me that he found one wing had been reassembled two degrees out of true.

On another occasion we were night flying. On my approach I found myself sinking inexorably below the glide path. I had to pour on full power just to reach the numbers on the end of the runway. Just before touchdown I felt a clunk. We discovered afterwards that the airbrakes were not retracting fully, so the best of the lift on the wings was being dumped. The clunking sound was my wheels catching the top strand of a barb wire fence around the perimeter of the airfield; luckily my undercarriage proved stronger than the fence or this story might have become posthumous.

Our training continued with many interesting tests to our judgement and ingenuity, such as air-to-air interceptions and firing on a towed drogue, air-to-sea canon firing and rocket launching.

One choice story was when the squadron came to visit their newly qualified civil pilot in my first civil job flying tourists around Blackpool Tower in a Dragon so old it was a prototype for the old de Havilland Rapide; G-ACIT was older than me. The Dragon and Rapide were affectionately known throughout the trade as the cloth bombers because of their plywood and stretched canvas construction.

The boys piled into the squadron commander's SS type Jaguar and two other cars and drove to Squires Gate looking for mischief. I, and the young lady who sold the tickets, were kidnapped into several local pubs and a riotous time was had by all.

The next day my squadron commander, Pete Rougier, called to say he had found the young lady's handbag carelessly left in his car and that he would return it that afternoon. I told the young lady that Pete was coming with her handbag and she seemed very pleased. At about 3.30 p.m. a formation of four Attackers appeared overhead the airfield and made a textbook landing. They folded their wings and taxied around the perimeter track until they stopped opposite the desk where the young lady sold her tickets. The leader's hood rolled back and an arm came out waving the handbag, which the astonished young lady accepted with a curtsy. The formation then left Squires Gate in the same flashy way as it arrived. The ticket young lady was enormously impressed with the Navy, and luckily I was the only one left behind for her to exercise her flabbergasted gratitude.

The RNVR Squadrons were all disbanded in 1957 due to defence cuts, we were all put on the reserve list for five years and I forgot all about the Navy. Years later I had just moved into a new house two weeks previously when a letter arrived from the Admiralty informing me that my five years as a reserve had been duly served and I was a free agent. What astonished me about the Navy was that they must have tracked my every address in the interim; there must have been at least six. As I have already said, the Royal Navy is a fearsomely efficient organization.

CHAPTER 2

Airlines: Short Haul

My Blackpool job ended with the tourist season and next I got some practical airline flying experience with Wally Ryde who had a job with a firm called Federated Fruit. Wally was always willing to take a co-pilot because his Anson's under-carriage had to be hand cranked to both the up and down positions. This chore required something like 250 turns of the hand crank and took several minutes to perform. Wally's job was to fly his Anson from Liverpool to Dublin, load up with Irish mushrooms and fly back. Some Scouse wag in the control tower quickly renamed the company Air Fungus, an appellation that was later more famously applied to Aer Lingus Irish International Airways, but Wally Ryde's mush-room express was the true origin of the sobriquet.

Over the next couple of months I managed to get the hang of what the CAA were after in the instrument rating and so, in January 1956, I was now qualified to reapply to BOAC.

I was accepted by BOAC but their next training course was in May. I was twenty-two, newly married with a pregnant wife and so broke I had to accept an immediate job in February with Cambrian Airways of Cardiff. I had a de Havilland Rapide and a Dove on my licence, both of which Cambrian operated and they may have been impressed that I flew in for interview in a Vampire. I had intended to dump Cambrian and take up BOAC's offer in May, but Cambrian proved such decent people, I couldn't do it. So, by fluke and financial necessity, I became an independent pilot, one of the underclass of British aviation, as opposed to a corporation (BOAC or BEA – British European Airways) fat cat. If this sounds like sour grapes, don't be misled, it is; but bear in mind that over thirty-six years I flew nearly twice the hours of my corporation colleagues for roughly half the money and pension, so maybe a little envious dyspepsia is forgivable.

Cambrian operated scheduled services around the south-west and I spent two enjoyable years flying to Paris, the Channel Islands, London, Belfast, Liverpool, Bristol and Southampton. My favourite trip was Bristol–Southampton–Paris in a Dove. The Dove is a superb eight-seat mini-airliner with all the equipment of much larger machines.

With no co-pilot you had to be very organized to get the job done correctly. Most enjoyable was the superb lunch at the Aerogarde at Le Bourget that opened my eyes to the pleasures of good food after years of food rationing in austerity Britain. I was having my lunch in Paris – I was really living! Many famous celebrities chose this press-free backdoor route for their trysts in Paris, but this was nobody's business but their own. I also got the DC3 Dakota on my licence and flew it as a co-pilot.

If Captain W.E. Johns based his Biggles character on a living pilot, then Cambrian's chief pilot, Geoff Perrott made the grade. Geoff was ex-RAF, tall, slim and easy-going, complete with dashing moustache. On one trip he and I had night-stopped in Belfast and the following morning was a typical shitty Northern Ireland clamp. The cloud base was eight-eighths of soggy stratus allegedly at 200 feet. The whole day looked and felt more like living inside a waterfall. Geoff was flying and, almost as soon as we were airborne, we were flying solely by instruments. Geoff pointed to the starboard oil pressure gauge, which was vacillating wildly (one of the cylinder heads had blown off). Geoff had the throttle closed, the fuel cut off and the engine feathered before I could say 'What's that?'

Single-engine operation in a fully laden, performance unclassified, Dakota is best glossed over, but Geoff inched us up to 1,500 feet like an alpine climber up a vertical ice cliff while I arranged for an immediate return with a GCA approach and landing.

A Ground Controlled Approach by radar is only as good as its operator who has to interpret two blips on two radar screens, one for azimuth (direction) and another for glide slope (height). He has to communicate his interpretation of the situation to the pilots over the radio; GCA was more of an art than a science. Our controller turned us downwind and then onto finals. At this point the quality of the pilot enters the equation. A GCA approach is also only as good as the pilot who needs to fly more smoothly and accurately than the DC3 was designed for to make the controller's manipulation of two radar blips as easy as possible. To be personal about it, my life was now relying on the interpretive performance of two mere human beings. Geoff Perrott was more than up for it, as I am here to confirm. I was never so relieved when we saw watery approach lights at two hundred feet in a downpour with the windscreen wipers going flat out and a rain-blurred runway in sight. Biggles could not have done it better and I was aware that I had just witnessed a classic example of above-average performance under extreme pressure with nothing to lose except your life. Geoff Perrott was my template for captaincy for the rest of my career.

Shortly after this time the ILS (Instrument Landing System) began to be fitted as standard, which made bad weather less of a trauma. The ILS transmitted two signals calibrated to indicate whether the aircraft was left or right of the centre line and above or below the glide path to levels of accuracy unique at that time.

The ILS was like a GCA, but it cut out the middle man and removed the pilot's perennial nightmare of getting caught out by fog with no hope of finding a runway. If you were seriously caught out you could always follow the needles all the way down and at least you would crash on the end of the runway with no trees or houses in the way of an expensive deceleration.

A special DC3 memory was a charter to Linz to pick up some of those Hungarians who had escaped their communist regime in the 1956 uprising. John Gibson, a war veteran Halifax pilot, was the captain. Coming out with full tanks and a full load we ran into 60 knot headwinds, which reduced our groundspeed to 80 knots. Then we picked up ice on the wings and our airspeed was reduced to 90 knots. Our groundspeed was something ridiculous; we could see cars overtaking us on the autobahn beneath. It was embarrassing. The Hungarians must have wondered what they had escaped into.

My progress in civil aviation so impressed the members of my squadron that Bill Brennen, Don Baines and Dougie Croll followed my example, while from the 37 RNVR course John Nokes, John Kitchen, Ian MacDade, Dave Brister, John McDonald, Ian Whitton and Terry Kemp also followed suit; so the Government got their money's worth out of us in the long run.

There are two types of airline pilot, long haul and short haul. Short haul pilots love the hurry and scurry of landings and take-offs. All they want to do all day is dart about the sky like bluebottles coming down frequently to uplift more fuel and change the passengers. If they have more than twenty minutes at top of climb they get altitude sickness. Long haul pilots want to fly to somewhere interesting, stop around for a couple of days, have a few parties, hire a car and see the sights.

All pilots, long or short haul, love landings. There is something orgasmic about lowering several hundred tons of engineering artwork back to earth as lovingly as a groom on a honeymoon. If you get it right there comes a deep satisfaction from producing the oink-oink sound that two protesting tyres make as they are eased from zero into the hundred miles per hour rotation of landing speed.

Although I couldn't have known it at the time, I was an instinctive long haul pilot, so I left delightful Cambrian Airways for a command on a Viking and the promise of a command on the DC4. The DC4 was a heavy, four-engine eighty-four seat long haul airliner that consumed me with challenge, ambition and lust; although it embarrasses me to admit that I once proselytized 'Where on earth are you going to find eighty-four people who all want to go to the same place on the same day?'

Independent Air Travel was owned by Marian Kozubski, a Polish ex-Bomber Command pilot who had survived two tours on Lancasters. Whatever else he was or was not, Kozubski must go down in aviation history as one of the founders of the subsequently massive inclusive tour industry.

After the war, civil aviation legislation stated categorically that BEA and BOAC were the chosen instrument for all UK air operations and they were accorded a complete monopoly of airline activity.

However, there were scraps these two weren't interested in, such as trooping contracts that moved the military between the dwindling outposts of the British Empire; also the corporations were not greatly interested in freight that involved the use of the entire aircraft without any passengers whatsoever. Kozubski noticed a clause in the legislation that independent airlines could fly passengers, provided that the entire aircraft was chartered. This loophole spawned the foundation of the inclusive tour market. Kozubski operated the airline, and his partner, Hughie Green, of BBC fame, founded a company called Skytours. Skytours advertised for the passengers and chartered the whole aircraft. Together they, and other copycat entrepreneurs, were becoming so successful that the corporations were calling foul and raising every objection they could think of – but Kozubski always found a sidestep, which was hugely irritating to officialdom. For example, customs would only allow the aircraft to uplift enough duty free for two packets of cigarettes and a half bottle of spirits per passenger. Kozubski's solution was to also uplift freight. This freight was invariably cases of booze and cigarettes and loaded into the cabin. As soon as the aircraft was outside British airspace, the freight was broached and the passengers could buy as much duty free as they wanted.

I was checked out on the Viking by Pete Souster. The Viking was a challenge, being very tricky to land nicely as she had obviously evolved from the kangaroo. We spent several weeks flying around a European winter visiting dozens of places I had not seen before. Theoretically, we were based in Hamburg, but we spent a lot of time going to Spain from Copenhagen, Gothenburg and Helsinki flying Scandinavians to Spain to escape their sun-starved suicidal winters.

Spain was still a foreign country in those days and Alicante and Malaga were gravel fields full of three foot high weeds and thistles that made it tricky to judge where the ground was. Majorca, I recall, had some very good night clubs. I was particularly fascinated by the gender elegance of flamenco.

I was duly checked out and my first trip in command was a charter to Beldringe. My first command problem was we couldn't find Beldringe on any map or navigational supplement. After a panic we discovered it was the local name of the airfield for Odense in Denmark, home of Hamlet's castle.

I really enjoyed flying around Europe because it was such a challenge going to strange airfields for the first time and needing to be bloody careful as I was not familiar with many of them or the local terrain. There were mountains all over Europe that were higher than the unpressurized Viking was allowed to fly so I did a lot of preparation.

This is not as hair-raising at it sounds. By law, all aircraft are required to carry a set of up-to-date aeronautical maps that show the local terrain and the approved routes around or across any mountains in the locality, together with the minimum safe altitude, which was also clearly listed. Also we carried maps of these approved routes and all the radio aids that defined them, so, as long as you did your home-work, you had all the necessary information to plan a safe route considering any mountainous terrain and the reported weather.

Kozubski's methods of finding ways around restrictive legislation became increasingly annoying to those bureau-crats whose task was to implement the corporations' mono-poly and many attempts were made to curb his free-spirited exuberance, but Kozubski always wriggled out of trouble. He had a completely different approach to serviceability than the industry norm because he had got back to base so many times with bits of aircraft shot off and this attitude pervaded the airline; as far as Marian was concerned the CAA were the new Nazis. Marian's pilots were an immensely practical bunch of Second World War survivors who were heroes as far as I was concerned. Whatever the obstacle, they found a way through and got the job done – like they were used to when the payload was bombs. For example, in those days you could cancel all air traffic control procedures by electing to fly by visual flight rules, known as VFR. VFR was possible in at least five miles' visibility and 1,000 feet clear of cloud. It meant that you were prepared to guarantee collision avoidance by keeping a good look out. Even at the airspeeds and traffic density of the times, it was a barely practical procedure but would be impossible with today's jet closing speeds of 1,000 miles per hour. It was a procedure that we used a lot to cut corners. I think it's fair to say we were a cowboy outfit with a tendency to resist the prevailing trends in the interests of the profit we needed to make to survive, whereas the corporation attitude was financed by the bottomless public purse. It was not a level playing field. Our philosophy was beginning to worry the CAA as they tried to direct a novice industry into the ways of improved safety.

Since I was in the company of pilots who had survived being shot at while I was still in short pants, and had medals to prove it, I was influenced by my peers, but my disquiet began to grow. I didn't mind struggling with an occasional unserviceability, but when I entered a quite serious defect in the technical log and flew the same aircraft a week later with the same defect being carried forward indefinitely, I began to get vocal. One aircraft had such a poor en route radio, the only way to get through was to go by VFR or pretend you had had a radio failure, and then follow the failed radio procedure until you got to destination. The radio failure procedure was that the aircraft would follow the flight plan as filed, without being able to confirm with the various en route air traffic controls that you were where the flight plan said you ought to be or even that you were there at all. (Flight plan: a document filed by the crew with the air traffic control agency, which listed the call sign of the aircraft, its captain and the number of souls on board. The plan itemized the route and altitude the pilot proposed to fly and on filing the flight plan in the airport operations office the plan would be telexed to all the air traffic control centres involved in processing the flight.)

The radio failure procedure itself was still theoretical and involved a lot of trust in the quality of these air traffic control centres who were themselves in the process of development. I did it once from necessity, but was not prepared to do it again. I was put under some pressure to comply and felt obliged to write a letter of protest to the Ministry. This was not the wisest move of my career because, a few days later,

Pete Maygar crashed his Viking freighter into some houses in Southall while attempting to return to Heathrow on one engine. The crew were all killed, as were some householders. The Ministry inspectors girded their loins for the *coup de grâce*.

I was subpoenaed to the inquest where I was supposed to turn whistle-blower. In court I had to think on my feet. I could do the right thing, but I would never get another job in civil aviation ever again, so I fended off the loaded questions. I still feel badly about this lack of moral fibre, but not too bad because, in those days, good captaincy was all about survival in the real world and I was the only one who cared about my own best interests.

The company was wound up after getting a terrible slating in the accident report.

Aviation**Safety***Network*

an exclusive service of **Flight Safety Foundation** www.flightsafety.org

Status:	
Date:	02 SEP 1958
Time:	06:32
Type:	Vickers Viking
Operator:	Independent Air Travel
Registration:	G-AIJE
C/n / msn:	127
First flight:	1946
Crew:	Fatalities: 3 / Occupants: 3
Passengers:	Fatalities: 0 / Occupants: 0
Total:	Fatalities: 3 / Occupants: 3
Ground casualties:	Fatalities: 4
Airplane damage:	Written off
Location:	5 km (3.1 mls) NE of London Airport (LHR) (United Kingdom)
Phase:	Initial climb
Nature:	Cargo
Departure airport:	London-Heathrow Airport (LHR/EGLL), United Kingdom

The Viking aircraft departed London at 05:54 GMT for a flight to Nice, Brindisi, Athens and Tel Aviv. Some 15 minutes later, engine trouble forced the crew to return to London. Though clearance had been given to descend to 3,000 feet, the crew was not able to maintain this altitude and kept descending until it crashed.

PROBABLE CAUSE: 'The aircraft was allowed to lose height and flying speed with the result that the pilot was no longer able to exercise asymmetric control. The conduct of the pilot and the whole course of events outlined were contributed to by the deliberate policy of this Company, which was to keep its aircraft in the air and gainfully employed regardless of the regulations or of the elementary requirements which should enjoin consideration for the conditions of working of its employees or the maintenance of its aircraft. Any responsibility of the captain is to be viewed in the light of his position as an employee upon whose shoulders an intolerable burden was placed.'

Sources:
ICAO Accident Digest, Circular 59-AN/54 (202-210)

This information is not presented as the Flight Safety Foundation or the Aviation Safety Network's opinion as to the cause of the accident. It is preliminary and is based on the facts as they are known at this time.

[legend] [disclaimer]

copyright 1996-2007 Aviation Safety Network
record last updated: 2007-04-15

(Reproduced courtesy of The Aviation Safety Network)

Having mentioned the radio failure procedure, some readers may be interested to know how the air traffic control system works.

When passenger flying began after the end of the First World War, it was immediately obvious that a system was needed to stop aircraft bumping into each other in poor visibility when they couldn't see while flying in the fog of cloud or at night.

The solution established a quadrantal height convention. Every aircraft flying on a course between north and east would fly at any odd thousands of feet (e.g. 5,000 feet). Aircraft flying between east and south would fly at any odd thousands of feet plus five hundred (e.g. 5,500 feet). Aircraft flying between south and west would fly at any even thousands of feet (e.g. 6,000 feet) and those flying between west and north would fly at any even thousands of feet plus five hundred (e.g. 6,500 feet).

The Quadrantal Height System

Magnetic track	000°–089°	090°–179°	180°–269°	270°–359°
Height (feet)	3,000	3,500	4,000	4,500
	5,000	5,500	6,000	6,500
	7,000	7,500	8,000	8,500

And so on upwards. So aircraft flying in opposite directions would always be separated by a thousand feet, which is more than adequate.

The inadequacy of this convention was that you could still collide with another aircraft that was at the same height and coming at you at an 89° angle. At any speed, an 89° angle collision would be just as fatal as one that was head on. As air traffic increased, further refinement became necessary.

Technology was very primitive and radio was the only aid available. A system was established that, in order to keep aircraft apart, they would be gathered into streams called airways, like roads in the sky. These roads would be defined by NDBs – Non Directional (Homing) Beacons. When used together with the compass and an intelligent assessment of the effect of drift caused by the prevailing wind, NDBs could provide accurate directional information in relation to a known geographical position.

The pilot is responsible for ensuring an accurate track maintenance and the air traffic controllers would use the pilot's position reporting to sequence aircraft safely along these airways using the position reports. The paradox was that to keep aircraft safely apart, the system brings them together into corridors so they can be sequenced by a remote third party over the radio.

With aircraft streamed into an airway by the quadrantal height convention, any aircraft coming in the opposite direction must be 1,000 feet above or below. Aircraft crossing an airway are legally required to cross at right angles, which meant that crossing traffic would either be 500 feet above or below any aircraft on the airway.

Aircraft flying down the airway at the same height were kept apart by sequencing, one every twenty minutes organized by the air traffic control service from the position reports over the radio. The gross inefficiency of this system is that each airborne aircraft occupies and reserves a slab of airspace that is ten miles wide, 2,000 feet thick and, at today's speeds, 160 miles long. Present day air traffic control has evolved from this clumsy system. Radar arrived and increased the efficiency, but the major cause of delay is congestion caused by the twenty-minute sequencing in the en-route portion of the trip where radar coverage is not available.

If an air traffic control system was being constructed today, with the benefit of today's technology explosion, it would be very easy to evolve a system that would be twenty times more efficient. Recently, I proposed such a system that was a refinement and extension of the quadrantal height system that, together with the incorporation of some twenty-first century technology, would allow air traffic control to become an automatic function of the autopilot.

The chairman of the Air Traffic Study Group of BALPA (British Airline Pilots' Association) described my idea as futuristic. This was obviously an opinion of someone who was completely undazzled by the flying developments from the Wright brothers' first powered flight to the moon landing in sixty-six years.

The Guild of Air Traffic Controllers were more realistic. Their opinion was that there was probably too much money already invested in the current system to allow for any change, even for a twentyfold improvement.

I read an article in *The Times* that Boeing was investigating the possibility of mass producing a vehicle that was a combined car and aircraft. I reasoned that if road congestion was to be transferred into the skies, since air traffic control was already overloaded, it was obvious that the only solution was a system that was more efficient and an automatic function of the autopilot with no human involvement at all. I wrote two letters to the CEO of the Boeing subsidiary concerned with a complete description of the idea. Either these both went astray or she didn't find the idea worth any acknowledgement. It seems normal in the human condition that innovation is blindly defended from any challenge to the status quo.

With the collapse of Independent Air Travel I was on the dole the whole of that winter until Marian Kozubski's next company was relaunched the following spring as BlueAir with all the usual suspects. There were some interesting trips. Bill Evans and I shared a tour to the Holy Land via Munich, Athens, Belgrade and Istanbul. With so many different countries to visit we took Jim Collins as steward. Jim was a cockney who could speak every language under the sun using his hands and facial expressions, an invaluable talent for dealing with the local agents, catering et cetera.

The passengers were touring Americans so we had time to do some sightseeing. The Acropolis and Jerusalem stand out in my memory. We were having dinner in Tel Aviv when suddenly all the men in sight put down their knives and forks, got up and left. Apparently there was a coded message on the radio calling for full mobilization because some Arabs tanks were straying too close to the border.

On another trip, coming out of Tenerife bound for Tangier, after a couple of hours there was no sign of the Moroccan coast, so I checked the co-pilot's navigation and found he had forgotten to apply the 12° variation correction to the compass course and we were in danger of missing Africa altogether. I did a rapid readjustment, and we diverted to Seville. We take all these destinations for granted today, but in the late fifties, they were all incredibly exotic and to see them all was exactly what I wanted from my life.

I got my Group 1 (Captain) Rating on the DC4 and a memorable trip to Hong Kong via Rangoon with Brian Howes.

Neither of us had ever been to Hong Kong and we arrived at about 8 p.m. for our first approach onto the famous runway 13 with its infamous chequerboard approach. Air traffic control was somewhat surprised that we had arrived at night without being familiar with Hong Kong's special procedures, but we got a most helpful controller who talked us down.

The infamous chequerboard approach consisted of radar vectors to Green Point NDB, continuing beyond on a set track until you could see the floodlit chequerboard in front of you. You then had to aim straight at the chequerboard, descending to six hundred feet as if planning to hit it. When you were so close you couldn't stand it any longer you made a sharp right turn and looked for the runway threshold, which would be found somewhere under the starboard wing. As one flight engineer said, the chequerboard approach stretched his belief in pilots. The next morning, when we saw what we had done the previous night in the dark, we went back and had a couple more beers.

As it was our first visit to Hong Kong we naturally went out for refreshments. In one bar I suddenly began to feel very strange. With a sailor's instinct I tacked back to the hotel with my condition deteriorating very fast. I staggered up to my room and just made the bed before it all went dark. I've never experienced anything like that before, or since, and I can only suspect that someone had slipped me a Mickey Finn to get to the company money, which we were obliged to carry as cash to pay for landing fees and agent's handling charges as credit cards had yet to be invented.

BlueAir collapsed at the end of the season, the second bankruptcy of my career. I was out of work, with a wife, two boys and a mortgage to upkeep. I vowed I would never let that happen again and subsequently always pursued a policy of having a second job up my sleeve. Desperate for a job, I heard that Airwork at Bournemouth Hurn were looking for a commercial pilot for a contract with the Atomic Energy Authority to fly personnel from Harwell to Manchester in a Rapide. Airwork were also flying Sea Furies and Meteors at Hurn for various Navy contracts, so I was precisely qualified for the job.

While on the dole the previous winter I had passed the exams for flight navigator, so when Freddie Laker's Air Charter advertised in *Flight* magazine for navigators for their DC4 route to Adelaide, Australia, I applied.

I pointed out that if they gave me the flying hours to complete the nav licence they would get a navigator and a Group 1 DC4 pilot as well. With two Group 1 pilots on board, the new maximum duty day limitations could be extended to 20(?) hours, which is useful in a long haul operation as cover for unexpected delays. The chief pilot, Ernest Jennings, thought it was a good idea and so I was transferred to Air Charter, which was also part of the Airwork Group.

I could have happily flown the Adelaide route for the rest of my life for many reasons (see map on last page of plate section). First, the route itself was 13 eight-hour legs from Southend to Benghazi, to Aden with a transit stop at Wadi Halfa, to Karachi, to Colombo, to the Cocos Islands in the middle of the Indian Ocean, to Perth in Western Australia and to Adelaide in South Australia. Then a repeat back home with Malta substituted for Benghazi. Because we were carrying rocket components for the Blue Streak missile we were not permitted to overfly Egypt outbound, but we were empty coming back and Malta was quicker. The apparent dog-leg to Karachi was because the DC4 didn't quite have the range for Aden–Colombo direct, however, coming home empty we could generally manage the short cut.

On the route, I was fascinated by the fact that the local inhabitants got browner and browner with each sector until Wadi Halfa, where they were purple, then they got lighter and lighter until we reached mainly white Australia.

On one trip, we were in the middle of the Sahara heading for Mount Uweinat, which defined the south-west corner of Egypt. I was taking a drift sight and lining up some dots on the ground when I suddenly realized the dots were moving. Looking more carefully, I could see it was a camel train. A camel train in the middle of the Sahara Desert! They were surrounded by sand dunes and about two hundred miles' walk from anywhere, with no water in sight.

The Adelaide route involved 115 flying hours out of the 30-day maximum allowance of 120 and took 14 days. So the next 16 days had to be days off, because, if the company used you for anything at all in the interim, it would reflect mid route into the next Adelaide trip. Theoretically, you could fly a world record of 1,440 hours each year having six months off on full pay!

A DC4 crew consisted of two pilots, three if they needed the extended duty day, a navigator and a radio operator. For the Adelaide route we carried a ground engineer whose job was to keep the aeroplane serviceable. He had to remain on the aircraft to act as a security guard for our top-secret cargo. The engineer was also in charge of catering and the good ones would start a stew pot after take-off. Because of the reduced pressure at altitude, the stew would boil at a much lower temperature and the potatoes would take hours to cook, so the smell of good cooking would pervade the cockpit and tantalize us for hours on end until it was ready and we would all get a big bowl for a late lunch. Hot food on an aeroplane! Whatever next?

Each leg was mostly in daylight, so we flew for eight hours then went to a hotel or Government Rest House for dinner and a good night's sleep. The Government Rest Houses were a leftover from the days of Empire and provided a good standard transit accommodation for those entitled to use them.

The take-offs from Wadi Halfa in temperatures in excess of 40°C were, like the Scottish play, not spoken about. It took ages to struggle up to 10,000 feet and nobody wanted to be the one to find out if it could be done on three engines.

Aden was a shopper's paradise being full of cheap Japanese radios, cameras and 8mm cine cameras. The crew regulars on the route had a shopping list for their friends and girl-friends in Cocos and Australia where such luxury items were unavailable.

We didn't see much of Karachi city as we stayed in a Government Rest House near the airport so as to be able to depart in the cool of early morning.

In Colombo we stopped in *The Mount Lavinia Hotel*, a hotel that came close to being my idea of perfection. It was a colonial gem set right on a beach lined with palm trees. The ebony floors were so highly polished you could see your face, and there were numerous gift shops selling exotic jewels of every type and colour. It was a treat just to be there at the company's expense.

After Colombo the navigation of the long crossing over the Indian Ocean to find a small island in the middle was the most interesting job in the aeroplane and a fascinating challenge. The navigator's table was known as The Lost Properly Department.

Astro-navigation (by the stars) is not as complicated as you might suppose. Except for the sun, moon and the planets, the heavens are full of thousands of stars whose positions are permanently fixed. The Earth rotates inside these thousands of fixed points of light whose positions are catalogued in the *Nautical Almanac* providing the astronomical equivalent of latitude and longitude called declination and hour angle. Declination is precisely similar to latitude whereas hour angle is registered from 0 to 24 hours because the Earth rotates once every 24 hours. If a known star was to pass precisely over your head, by looking up that star's declination and hour angle you could quite simply resolve your position. If the declination of this star was 35° south, the aircraft's position must be somewhere on 35° south latitude. By converting the star's listed hour angle to 360° notation you would arrive at a longitude.

This is the cunning bit. What if your known star didn't pass precisely overhead, but its sextant altitude measured 89° 00′, one degree of arc away from directly overhead? Since one minute of arc equals one nautical mile on the Earth's surface (by definition) then our position would be somewhere on the circle that had a radius of sixty miles around the Earth position of our known star. We wouldn't know exactly where we were on that circle until we obtained another circle from another star. Where those two circles crossed would give two possible positions. Three star circles would fix our position exactly. With refinements, this is basically all astro-navigation does.

The standard ship's sextant requires a visible horizon from which to measure the angle of the star, moon or planet that you want to use. At sea it was traditional to get a good latitude at midday as the sun crossed due south (or north) of you and also a good three-star fix at dawn and dusk when you could see both the brightest stars and the horizon. While a good fix twice a day in twilight was adequate for shipping, an aircraft needs a position fix at least every hour because an aircraft is directly affected by wind and jet streams of over a hundred miles an hour could put an aircraft the same hundreds of miles off track in the same hour. So the bubble sextant was designed for aircraft use and, since a good horizon is not available at night and rarely visible from an aircraft by day, the horizontal is defined from the vertical by a bubble that floats at the precise apex of a circular vessel of oil and works like a spirit level. The design allows the navigator to see the star being measured in the middle of this dimly illuminated bubble.

On the Colombo to Cocos sector, since we were flying by day over the ocean, the only navigational aids available were bubble sextant altitudes of the sun and clinging on to track by very frequent sightings from the drift sight. The drift sight measures the angle between where the aircraft is pointing and its directional movement over the Earth. The difference between the two is caused by the winds pushing the aircraft sideways. By measuring the drift angle and applying it to the required track, the aircraft can at least be sure that it is roughly staying on the track – going in the right direction – that will ultimately lead it to where it is trying to go.

The particular problem of the Colombo–Cocos sector was that it was daytime, so the only chance to get a good fix on the route was to catch the sun at midday as it passed overhead and crossed your meridian. By calculating the times, you could get three intercepts, which would give you a good three-position line running fix; but you had to be quick and accurate because this event window was only twenty minutes' wide.

I heard one horror story where the crew reckoned they must be about an hour out of Cocos, so they switched on the NDB, and sure enough the needle showed that Cocos was dead ahead. However, they were somewhat confounded when the needle suddenly switched direction and showed Cocos was now immediately behind them. This opened up a whole menu of panicky likelihoods. Was the instrument telling lies? Had they unknowingly picked up a tailwind? Should they ignore the needle and press on towards the dead reckoning position of the Cocos Islands one hour further on? This could prove a ghastly blunder if the needle was telling the truth. The problem was resolved by an Aussie voice from Cocos tower who called over the radio, 'G'day Alpha Bravo, we heard you pass overhead. Do you mind telling us where the blazes you think you're going to now?'

Nowadays the INS (Inertial Navigation System, see below) does the job better, with remarkable accuracy.

In Perth and Adelaide we were most welcome visitors coming all the way from London, which in those days was on another planet; particularly to the nurses from the Adelaide General Hospital who were extremely professional and always willing to come to the nearest bar in their off duty time to help us with our 'alcohol addiction problem'. We would take back bottles of Australian wine from the Barossa Valley. Back home, people sneered at the idea of Aussie wine, but our palates insisted it was very agreeable stuff, particularly the sherry. But what did we know? I also brought back two examples of Aussie Fine Art. One was a tee shirt emblazoned with 'POMMIE BASTARDS', a *cri de coeur* from some would-be who became more widely known as Dame Edna Everidge and another was a record of 'Tie me kangaroo down sport' by another wannerbe called Rolf Harris. I regret to admit that the export of the Rolf Harris phenomena to England may have been my fault.

I just loved Australia and over the years wrote scores of letters to Qantas begging for a job. One joker suggested that they wouldn't have me because I didn't have a qualifying criminal record; to a Liverpudlian, to be accused of not having a criminal record is a gross insult to your street-credibility.

We lost the Adelaide contract to Eagle Airways' bigger and faster DC6s and I was posted to Southend-on-Sea to fly the Bristol Freighter.

As a Bristol Freighter captain in the newly formed British United Airways based in Southend, the task, in the days before the Channel Tunnel, was carrying cars and freight across the Channel. It was a very slick operation. Each shift was flying either four Calais, three Ostends or two Rotterdams.

On turnaround the nose doors would be opened, a car ramp would be positioned and three cars could be unchained, driven off by specialist car marshallers, then three more cars would be driven in, chained down and you could turnaround inside twenty minutes.

You got a lot of practice at landings, and as the weather deteriorated you got to assess your own personal minima to the nearest inch; crosswind landings in particular. I will never forget one crosswind landing at Ostend. There was a squally gale blowing and we were right on limits. There was so much rain and drift I had to open the DV panel, an angled quarter light, to see the runway because we were coming in practically sideways. The rain was pouring through the open DV, arcing over the pedestal and drenching our general manager, a Mr Lewindon, who was cadging a ride on the jump seat. Being high wing, you could land the Bristol 170 with quite remarkable wing-down angles so I touched down on the right wheel and gradually lowered the left wheel onto the ground but the problem was that we didn't decelerate a single knot and were slowly and inexorably drifting downwind to the runway edge at 90 knots. In desperation, just before we were going to go into the mud, I released the tailwheel lock and let her weathercock into the wind. The extraordinary thing was that we lost all the 90 knots going at 45° across the runway.

With such repetitious schedules there was a risk of monotony. It was a time when there was still space for characters. One captain used to buy three types of cigars in Ostend. He had a different one for Calais, Ostend and Rotterdam. He would light the appropriate one after take-off, and by assessing how much cigar was left, tell the co-pilot who was maintaining the lookout, to either report mid-Channel or top of descent. As he reached the end of his cigar he would put down the crossword, crack open the DV panel, the dog end would be tidily sucked out and he would release the autopilot, look ahead and land.

An unexpected blessing on the Rotterdam route was the arrival of Radio Caroline, the pirate radio ship that broadcast pop music from outside British territorial waters. The Establishment was outraged and demanded a good old Empire gunboat response, a lack of cool that ensured that a whole generation tuned into nothing else. Caroline was right on the Southend to Rotterdam track so the crews had professional excuses to listen to the latest pop music on the ADF (Automatic Direction Finder – a radio designed to receive the NDB, a legal requirement for en-route position reporting).

The summers were madly busy. I recall being in a BALPA posse going to see Freddy Laker, the owner of Air Charter, with a demand for at least one day off in ten. Freddy stuck a Cuban cigar in our mouths, poured some hundred-year-old brandy down our throats and told us to go away (although those were not the exact words he used). He said we would get all our days off all together in the off-peak winter. Since this was undeniable we came away empty handed. In those days an independent company that kept you on the payroll over the winter was a priceless bonus.

Besides the pleasure of handling aeroplanes, I was in flying to see the world, so in the quiet winters I used to volunteer for anything that was going. This policy had taken me for a winter flying the Bristol Freighter across the Cook Strait in New Zealand, a tour in Sierra Leone bush flying the diamond mines, and a spell flying the oil pipeline based at T2 in the middle of the Syrian Desert.

Four of us were detached to SAFE (Straits Air Freight Express) at Blenheim in New Zealand's South Island. SAFE's task was similar to the Channel Airbridge in that we connected the two Kiwi islands with a freight service much faster than the ferries. SAFE's check-out was thorough, and needed to be because the winds in the Cook Strait were often unbelievable. These southern hemisphere winds, famously known as the Roaring Forties, were squeezed through the Straits between the North and South Islands, and exaggerated as a result. Wellington Airport's runway was built on reclaimed land and stuck out into the bay. It was a bit like landing on an aircraft carrier. On a bad day the runway would be shielded from the wind by the mountains to the west, but as the storm increased the winds would sweep over the mountains and curve back down to flatten the water in the harbour. As the storm intensified, we would keep a weather eye on the sea and watch the wind flattened patch creep closer to the runway threshold. When the down-draught reached the threshold we would divert to Paraparaumu.

The problem with Paraparaumu was that it had rising ground to the east. We were diverting there because of excessive winds, so you were going downwind into rising ground in front of you with a downwind groundspeed increased by the 50 knots you were diverting for in the first place. With the rising ground threatening like falling down a mine shaft you had to start your turn onto finals from halfway down the runway because, by the time you were lined up with the threshold, the wind had blown you into a normal finals position. Paraparaumu diversions were a nail-biting experience.

New Zealanders must be the most natural and friendliest people on the planet, rugby excepted. The hotel moved us into a four-bedroom bungalow in anticipation of what would happen over Christmas. On our first weekend we were invited to a goat clearance trip. This involved a boat ride into the 'Sounds' (Sounds are New Zealand's equivalent of Norway's fiords, but less dramatic, being hilly rather than mountainous). I finished my flying detail in the early afternoon and went into the hall of our bungalow to find a .303 rifle leaning against the hall stand. Attached was a note saying 'You don't know me, but I hear you are going after goats this weekend. You probably don't have a gun, so borrow mine, and here's a box of shells.' I don't know of another place in the whole world where that could happen. I'm sure of this because I've told the rest of the world this story and they all agreed it is unique.

New Zealand in 1960 had some unique problems, which the Kiwis dealt with in very practical ways. If you wanted a house, you built one; likewise with boats. I learned to water ski in a homebuilt boat fitted with an old Ford engine that had only two speeds; full speed ahead and off. The pubs all closed at 6 p.m., so the first thing a newly married couple would buy was a wash boiler. This boiler was used exclusively for making beer and never saw any knickers or underpants (so they said). At that time in New Zealand there were good looking women and there were women who could make a good brew, a bloke had to decide his own order of priority.

Our Blenheim posting, in the days before the Marlborough Valley wine explosion, passed enjoyably with goat clearance trips (goats were grass-eating vermin that cost the farmers an equal number of sheep), pig hunts (root-eating pigs could utterly defoliate an island in a couple of years), night rabbit shoots and whitebait netting. There is no contest, New Zealand whitebait and Havelock's mussels are the best in the world washed down by the world-class Marlborough white wines.

There was a great coffee bar in Blenheim called *The Habit*. It was a great meeting place for all and sundry. I was talking to some guys one evening and they asked me if I played rugby. Modestly I mentioned that I had played a few times for Navy teams and the like. Great, they said. 'We are looking for a wing forward. It's just a social game against a bunch of local Maoris; should be a pushover.'

I had never even heard about the Hakka before, so initially I found the ritual charming, but when I registered the looks on their faces I felt a tremor of apprehension. I don't remember the final score, but I do remember the utter silence in the dressing hut after. It was the last game I ever played.

Christmas was not so much a moveable feast as a continuous one for the whole town. There was a huge stash of empty beer bottles by the front door, so, for a joke, we spread them out side by side around the bungalow. By New Year's Day we were starting on the third row.

My two other detachments involved conversion to the Twin Pioneer. Scottish Aviation's Twin Pioneer was a sixteen-seat short take-off and landing bush aircraft with a fixed under-carriage and tailwheel. It was powered by two Alvis Leonides radial engines. There were only three speeds to remember. She climbed at 90 knots, cruised at 100 and stalled at around 65. As you would expect in a bush aircraft, she was minimally equipped with VHF, HF and an ADF.

I passengered to Freetown, Sierra Leone, on BUA's (British United Airways) African Air Safari route for a six-month detachment with Sierra Leone Airways (SLA). The chief pilot, Ken Sheppardson checked me out on the aircraft and then I positioned to Lagos to do the ARB exam. Although Ghana had just become independent and Accra was a ferment of excitement, Nigeria was still part of the British Empire and had a Colonial Aviation Authority.

After the exam I positioned back to Freetown on a West African Airways DC3. What I remember about that trip is sitting next to an Israeli salesman who asked me why it was that in the French colonies the natives spoke perfect French, whereas in the British colonies the natives spoke pidgin English. I had to admit I could not explain this, but a seed had been sown, which germinated into a flicker of doubt about our self-satisfied British Empire.

SLA operated services up country from Hastings to Bo, Kenema and Yengema, the latter being the epicentre of the diamond mining industry. There was an NDB at Lunghi and Bo, but that was all. The rest was pure bush flying – you had to learn your trees because they were the only navigational help you could get in the rainy season.

The rainy season in Sierra Leone is an underwater experience just short of needing scuba gear; it rains like being under four well directed showers with your clothes on. Everything is damp. Everything in your wardrobe grows green mould and even the mosquitoes refused to go out in that kind of weather.

Bush flying is the ultimate test of practical flying. Without navigational aids you had to cling on to your landmarks and geography to get through. One day I was flying under an overcast tunnel up the valley that led to Yengema when suddenly the heavens open up like a burst dam – instant zero visibility. There was no option but to climb up to safety height, being very careful to keep straight. It was only safe because I knew my geography. Once on top of the cloud I had no option but to fly back to base.

On another occasion I stupidly left the HF switched on at Bo, and when I came back the battery was flat. I had to arrange with the local government works contractor to borrow two 12-volt lorry batteries, which I connected up in series to give the 24 volts I needed to get an engine going.

Although this account is about the gradual development of aviation, my flying experience and technique, flying taught me some personal lessons that were unique to my multi-national environment.

One day I was driving to work and passed through a village where most of our ground staff lived. Usually it was deserted, but on this day there was a huge crowd of people clamouring at the gates of the schoolhouse. I asked what was going on and was informed that these were parents trying to get their child into one of the limited places in the school. I was disgusted. We British had only been running Sierra Leone for two hundred years and we still hadn't managed to provide enough schooling for those who wanted it – as opposed to the UK where school is compulsory for everybody, like it or not.

My disgust with the Empire's inadequate performance was underlined one night at the local cinema. They were showing Lawrence Olivier's *Henry V*. We whites were in the balcony and the locals were in the stalls. What was so charming was the identification. The French were booed and hissed and the English cheered and clapped. At the start of the famous Agincourt battle scene the atmosphere from the stalls was stiflingly tense. There was a gasp as a thousand arrows were loosed into the sky and a tsunami of relief at the pandemonium it caused to the French cavalry. There was cheering when we won. That is the point. They considered they were British and were watching a part of their own proud heritage. I felt ashamed that our wealthy Empire took all their diamond wealth to London and didn't even build enough schools for those who wanted an education. What a tragedy that the Great British Empire upon which the sun never set, that gave Africa some kind of order, that policed the world, albeit in our own best interest, was lost because our upper class ruling Eton-Oxbridge twits were too superior to let the locals – who we were robbing blind, into our clubs and dining rooms – into our society, so naturally they couldn't wait to become independent.

I found Sierra Leonians to be cheerful, simple people. One day at Kenema a local came out of the bush. He was sort of dressed; I recall he had trousers, although there was no back to them. He said something to me that I didn't catch at first, but after a few attempts I realized that he was demanding a ride in 'de buzz-buzz lorry for go up'.

My houseboy was a Muslim called Musa. He was experienced and very capable. One day he asked to 'dash me five pounds to buy a new wife'.

There was a story going around up country, probably apocryphal, about a couple of new expatriates briefing their houseboy about dinner. The houseboy had a problem with cottage pie and they carefully explained the recipe.

After dinner they were well pleased and asked the houseboy for the same again tomorrow. 'Oh no, master', the boy complained. 'It took me all morning to chew dis much.'

My second tour in Freetown was after Sierra Leone had become independent. The airline was flying the bigger, faster Heron that I had suggested after my Cambrian experience. The detachment was highlighted by two incidents.

Lou Wilbur was our station engineer, but he was also qualified for running repairs to the Air Safari Viscounts that transited Lunghi on the way to Liberia. Lunghi International Airport, was on the other side of the Sierra Leone river estuary. Rather than take the long ferry passage, Lou had negotiated a deal with a local politician who owned a light aeroplane, a single seat Tipsy Nipper. Lou would maintain the Tipsy for free if he could borrow it to fly across to Lunghi to oversee the Viscount's transit. Lou needed the flying experience as he was building up his hours to get a commercial pilot's licence.

I was flying back to Hastings when I got a call from Lunghi ATC that they'd heard a rumour that the Tipsy had crashed near the airfield. I landed back as quickly as I could to be greeted by Lou's agitated mechanics who said they had seen the Tipsy crash and would take me to the scene.

The Tipsy was in a wadi close by; it was intact, but resting tail up and on its nose. Lou was still in the pilot's seat, or at least his body was. When he hit the ground he had snapped the seat harness, which had left him with enough momentum to crash his head through the Perspex hood. This had shattered, but left enough jagged edges to cut his head off. I found his head about twenty yards up the wadi. I had never seen a dead body before and Lou had driven me to work that morning. I was in a kind of shock and had this ridiculous impulse to pick up his head and stick it back inside his trunk, and maybe he would be okay.

The funeral was ghastly in the local church. It was rainy season and the grave was already overflowing with water so the coffin was floating. We had to pile rocks on top of it to make it sink so we could bury him.

Freetown is a hot, tropical musky city. I was there on my own and feeling so healthy you wouldn't believe it. After the hot sweaty air-condition free flight back to Hastings I would jump in the car and cool off at the beach. There I would lust after the wives and girlfriends in their bikinis. At night I would go down to the Cape Club and watch the girls dancing. The club had an idyllic setting on the beach and its focal point was a giant cottonwood tree around which a marble floor had been laid. There were two favoured dances. One was the local 'Highlife', a rhythmic shuffle around the cottonwood tree filled with coloured lights that cast a romantic glow on the dancers below. The waves murmured on the beach behind and inevitably there was blown sand on the marble that emphasized the rhythmic Highlife causing a hypnotic beat like a drum being scratched. The worst was the jive. Flared skirts were in and these would flare out in a complete circle like the Rings of Saturn, revealing the entire southern hemisphere of that most charming of planets below. I formed the impression that this was no accident, that women knew exactly what they were doing to the beer swilling moaners at the surrounding tables. There were never any spare women. They were all married or engaged or were the unapproachable and exotic daughters of the ambassador from some place or other in their beautiful saris. One thing I remember about that detachment was the steam escaping out of my ears. The Canadians call it a 'white out' when the sperm level rises above the eyebrows.

My departure from Sierra Leone was unexpected and accelerated. I was on the last leg of the day from Bo back to Freetown in the Heron. Lawyer McCauley, one of our best customers, was booked, but hadn't shown up yet. McCauley was a prickly, UK-trained lawyer of mixed blood who had had enough of the British and their exclusivity that excluded educated natives like himself from the newly formed independent government in favour of the naïve indigenous local chiefs. I waited as long as I decently could, then in consideration for the other passengers, decided to go without him.

I started the engines, and was just about to taxi away when I noticed the passenger door warning light come on and go off. I opened the cockpit door and saw Lawyer McCauley making towards an empty seat.

This opened up a whole menu of options. Legally, the load sheet was now incorrect, but this was bush flying, and since we were not overloaded, I continued the taxi and took off, amending the POB (passengers on board) over the radio.

We had a problem. Before independence the out stations were managed by ex-pat wives who only needed showing once, and who knew instinctively the difference between right or wrong. After independence the ex-pat wives had to be replaced by locals. The local station manager who now handled the turnaround at Bo must have known he was flouting CAA and company regulations, but he was institutionally tuned to the reality that CAA and company regulations did not apply in Africa where the powerful were concerned.

I called Lawyer McCauley to the cockpit and asked him if he had 'dashed' the station manager to put him on the aircraft, wanting to know just how reliable our manager was.

'You are accusing me of bribery,' he said.

'No I'm not,' I answered. 'I'm asking you if you did.'

The next day a writ was duly served to head office in which McCauley accused me of slander.

My position was that a question is not an accusation, a question which I, as captain of an aircraft and responsible for its safe and legal operation was fully entitled to ask. However, our lady barrister, an extraordinarily beautiful, Oxford-trained, Sierra Leonean, also of mixed race, advised that the local courts would be unable to handle such a fine distinction, and might be inclined to be partial anyway. She advised that I leave the country ASAP.

In between the Freetown detachments I did a relief sojourn at a pipeline station called T2 in the middle of the Syrian Desert because the contract pilot had reported sick. I positioned out to Beirut in an Alitalia Caravelle. I was impressed with the steward who served the passenger in front of me in German, myself in English and the passenger behind in French. I asked him how he knew which language to use without asking. 'Tailoring,' he replied.

In those days Beirut was the jewel of the Middle East. You could swim in the morning, ski in the afternoon, eat like a sheikh and club until dawn.

Next day I was driven through the mountains to Damascus to get a Syrian work permit and then on to T2, the main pumping station.

I had no idea that oil was pumped in pipes from Kirkuk in Iraq, hundreds of miles across the Syrian Desert to Banias on the Mediterranean coast for shipment around the world. This massive task involved building a series of pumping stations (T1, T2, T3 and T4) to move the oil westwards. My job was moving passengers and freight between these stations along this pipeline.

At one time each station involved the employment of scores of men who were housed in large messes similar to an Army or RAF Officer's Mess, but modernization and automation had reduced the manpower required to three: one European oilman to oversee the locals, and two others, myself and my engineer.

There is some element of the unreal in being on a pipeline station in the middle of the desert with just three of us in a huge two hundred-room mess. The resident oilman, inevitably, was a Scot. He used to move into one of the many vacant rooms every Monday morning. He would work like a demon all week to keep the oil flowing. On Saturday night he would enjoy the special steak dinner and retire to his room with a case of Scotch. For the rest of that night and the whole of Sunday we would hear nothing except singing, raucous laughter, bagpipes and the crack of smashing furniture. On Monday morning he would emerge from his wrecked room refreshed and, without a word of explanation, move into the room next door and work like a demon until the next Saturday. By the end of the month I was screaming to Jennings to get me out of there; no wonder the incumbent pilot on an eighteen-month contract went a bit strange.

Two incidents come to mind from that time. One of my tasks was to watch for signs of leaks in the pipe. This was the perfect excuse for low flying, which as every pilot knows is the best way to see the world. Several times I startled deer and desert foxes. On one trip, as I appeared over the brow of a hill, I surprised a large flock of sheep. Three dogs launched themselves out of the flock and fanned out in formation keeping between me and the sheep. It was of no concern of theirs how big an eagle I was, I was only going to get to their sheep over their dead bodies. It was the bravest thing I ever saw and this has remained for me as a benchmark for instinctive courage.

Another surprise was the large numbers of castles in that region. I had heard of the Crusades of course, but it never occurred to me that they stayed long enough to build castles every bit as intentionally permanent as Harlech or Windsor. I used to fly over a town called Palmyra, which had four clear quarters: the first was prehistoric, the second was an abandoned Roman quarter obvious from the Doric columns, the third a mediaeval quarter. The fourth quarter was modern and was the only part in use today. The idea of having enough space to just walk away from an area and start again in the next quadrant is foreign to the British experience.

In the heavy winter of 1963/4, when part of the Thames froze over, the chief pilot phoned and asked me to take a Twin Pioneer out to the Cape Verde Islands off the coast by Dakar with a view to selling her to a French Company. I was more than ready to escape from snowbound Britain.

Keith Sissons brought G-APLN aka 5-NABQ from Prestwick. I met him as he landed at Southend. Keith was not happy. He was blue with cold. Apparently, it had taken them several hours to find the aeroplane buried under a snowdrift at Prestwick. Keith's opinion of the aircraft was entirely four lettered. There was no fucking cockpit heating and the temperature had plummeted to minus sixteen in the cabin. As he handed her over he wished me the very best of British luck, which, as it turned out, was exactly what I was to need in trumps.

At some point I need to admit, if it isn't already obvious, that at that time I was a pilot with attitude. This attitude was that my job was to get the job done, that God invented problems for me to find solutions – a challenge that entirely

64

suited my high opinion of myself. I considered that, short of a wing falling off, I could handle anything.

I was completely in charge of the operation so I spent a couple of days gathering an inventory of useful en-route spares, sorting out the radios, getting the right HF frequencies for West Africa fitted and checked. HF (High Frequency) is a band of radio frequencies designed for long range. Long range is achieved by the fact that radio transmissions of these frequencies could be bounced round the Earth from the ionosphere. However, because the ionosphere can often have the uneven shape of the bottom of an egg box, the HF is not totally reliable. From previous experience I have always mistrusted the HF networks that replaced the specialist radio operators. It seemed to me that HF was perverse and only worked when you didn't need it. When you really needed it you spent hours trying to make contact with somebody, anybody. Often it seemed that only God was listening. Once, in Sierra Leone I got a relay of my flight details from Rangoon. What kind of communication system is that? However, clumsy though HF is, by repetition and persistence, you generally got through.

A Scottish Aviation engineer, Les Palmer, joined the crew whose task was to get the maintenance started in Dakar. Finally, we had done everything we could think of. I drew out a float of traveller's cheques to pay for landing fees, hotels et cetera, filed a flight plan and we set off. The first leg was to go to Paris Villacoublay, load up a spare engine and some more spares. Keith was right about the temperature, it was minus sixteen in the cockpit and I flew the sector with my cap and gloves on and my raincoat buttoned up to my neck.

Approaching Paris, the ADF froze on some useless frequency and I had to divert to Beauvais and make the approach using a rarely used and almost forgotten QDM cloud break procedure much to the amusement of Paris ATC. A QDM procedure involves requesting a series of homing bearings and using these to align with the runway to descend safely through the clouds. At Beauvais we fixed the ADF (it thawed out?) and continued on to Toussus-le-Noble. There was a spare engine waiting but nothing to lash it down with so we had to scrounge some rope. Having worked out the ideal position from the load and trim sheet, we removed a couple of rows of seats and lashed the engine down to my satisfaction.

As a last-minute addition, the French company asked me to take their new co-pilot with me so that he could be familiar with the aeroplane by the time we arrived. Hero was a young recently graduated Breton. Since weight was not a problem, we could take full tanks every sector, I was happy to oblige.

I had flown the route northbound from Freetown so I planned Paris to Biarritz, Seville, Casablanca, Las Palmas, Port Etienne, St Louis and Dakar. Each sector was about 400 miles – four hours at 100 knots without an autopilot is enough. I knew some good hotels and restaurants and could look forward to the temperature steadily rising as we went south.

Paris–Biarritz–Seville–Casablanca all went to plan. I took the three of us out to a slap-up meal each night, had a good breakfast and I bought some lunch boxes. En route, to keep warm, I stayed as low as the safety height permitted and by the time we got to Casablanca the cabin temperature was getting close to a respectable zero.

Next morning at Casablanca the weather forecast was wide open. The wind was slightly more favourable at lower altitudes, and since, at 100 knots, any help or hindrance from the wind is critical, I planned a descent to 3,000 feet after we crossed Safi on the coast, climbing higher for safety height as we crossed Fuerteventura in the Canaries.

We set off for Las Palmas. As we approached Safi I could see heavy cloud ahead. Since the temperature at 3,000 feet was hovering on zero and the Twin Pioneer was not equipped with anti-icing equipment, I tried to skirt around the weather, but, with the Atlas mountains looming to port, I was forced to land at Marrakech and reassess.

At Marrakech we discovered a serious problem. There were only two lifejackets. I spent two hours trying to buy one but there was no lifejacket shop at the airport. I tried to borrow one from the Air Maroc parked alongside, but they insisted they didn't have any to spare. It was a choice between dumping the Frenchman, Hero, to take his chances at getting a lift home or onwards to Dakar, or taking a risk. In desperation I made a fateful decision, in the unlikely event that we needed lifejackets, I was a strong swimmer (ex-lifeguard) and would have to make do with floatable seat cushions from the spare seats.

On the ground at Marrakech the weather quickly passed over revealing a gin clear sky out to the west. The revised weather forecast was again perfect and the winds were the same as ex-Casa. I was having the usual problems with the HF radio (nobody was replying), so I decided that we would press on to Las Palmas because the company had a radio engineer on station to service our West African Air Safari Viscounts, I could get any required re-tuning over-night and some experienced local advice about the most reliable frequencies. I made a new flight plan (see map on page 6 of the plate section). On crossing the coast I would track out to intercept a back bearing from Agadir, which would cut the corner and save a few more minutes.

I would fly parallel to the coast to abeam El Alouain, then island hop to Las Palmas where the assured VHF contact would make up for deficiencies in the HF. This way I would never be more than the legal thirty minutes' flying time from land without a dinghy.

I noticed in the Aerad Navigation Supplement that the NDB at Fuerteventura was HJ/OR (on during the day and on request at night), so I attached a plain language request on the flight plan for it to be operating between 2200 hours and midnight.

We took off into a pretty sunset where fate had obviously intended we should disappear without trace somewhere in the South Atlantic; but fate hadn't reckoned with the Williams luck.

Initially, all went as planned. I descended to 3,000 feet over the sea and intercepted the back bearing from Agadir. Unexpectedly, we ran into cloud, but since the desert temperature was now above zero, this wasn't an icing problem.

I had hoped that Hero would perform as autopilot so that I could keep a genuine plot to help renew my Flight Navigator's Licence, but he was a passenger, not legal flight crew, and it was well past his bedtime. After straying off course a couple of times, I found it easier to fly it myself. I got a groundspeed and distance off check along track from Sidi Ifni and I remember being relieved that the time was an even twenty minutes, so I didn't have to use the Dalton computer in the dark. The Dalton is a hand-held device used to measure the sideways drift angles caused by the wind.

We seemed to be having trouble getting abeam of the El Alouain NDB, which was swinging through thirty degrees on the bow, I was not receiving the requested Fuerteventura NDB at all and the Agadir back bearing had faded so I had nothing. At some point I began to get worried, nothing tangible, just instinct. Certain at least that I was still over the sea I descended to 1,500 feet, the safe height for the El Alouain area. We were still in the bottoms of the cloud, but I thought I could see something that looked like the lights of a city beneath. This was utterly impossible so I inched down a few feet more to get a closer look.

The cause of my worry was immediately obvious. I wasn't seeing a city, I was practically down into the sea and seeing phosphorescence being whipped up by a strong wind. The waves were mountainous and the drift unbelievable. With insufficient information whether to continue or turn back, I decided I needed some certainty of position so, figuring that Africa is too big to miss, I set a course for the coast in the vicinity of El Alouain, which should have been about twenty miles on my port side. I climbed to a revised safety height for the area and waited for an El Alouain transit. After an hour, nothing had happened; El Alouain NDB was still oscillating wildly ahead. I looked at the fuel gauges. If we didn't transit El Alouain soon, we weren't going to have enough fuel for Las Palmas! We were in trouble. I might have to divert to El Alouain (a daylight military airfield), raise them somehow, or worse, ditch in the sea as close to the coast as I dared. I decided it was time to make a Mayday. I was more angry than frightened at having got into such a ridiculous mess. I woke up Hero and Les Palmer and told them to listen because there was a problem.

The mnemonic for a distress call came readily to mind. 'Mayday, Mayday, Mayday. Golf Alpha Papa Lima November is en route Marrakech to Las Palmas and un-certain of position. We are diverting to El Alouain, course one three five degrees. Speed one hundred knots, Height three thousand feet QNH. We are uncertain of position and intend to land at El Alouain or ditch in the sea.'

'Ah,' said Hero, 'Somebody is in trouble, yes?'

I was forced to clarify, 'Yes. That was us.'

The first call was on the HF (long range). Nobody responded. You don't really ever expect to make a Mayday call, but when you do you at least expect to get a reply, and when you don't it is a very lonely experience. I tried again on VHF (short range) and got no reply. I was told later (unconfirmed) that an Iberia DC3 heard our Mayday but couldn't get a reply from us. I looked at the fuel gauges again. We would run out of fuel and ditch in the sea. Even if we survived the ditching we wouldn't last much longer after that. I reckoned I had about an hour left to live.

At that point we came out of cloud into a pale watery moonlight and I saw a light. A light meant civilization of some kind and whatever it was, El Alouain or not, I was going to have some. I dived down to it and saw it was a fishing boat being buffeted about in very heavy seas.

Subsequent back plotting was to reveal that the 100-knot GAPLN had encountered an unforecast 100-knot wind intense depression somewhere between a tornado and a hurricane and had been effectively stopped in its tracks. Luckily, I had diverted into the hurricane's eye, and there in the relative calm was more than unbelievably fortunate to find a fishing boat.

I recalled, from Fleet Air Arm briefings, the classic place to ditch is alongside a vessel at sea, but I was enough of a seaman to realize that no boat could easily manoeuvre in seas like that. I decided I would ditch a couple of miles ahead, so that, even if the boat didn't see us go down, in a few minutes she would hit us. I made a couple of low passes to wake them all up. We had no means of communication and my plan was to signal SOS with the landing light. However, fate was still pressing for a result, and for its final throw of my dice it arranged for the landing light to refuse to extend or illuminate. So my task now was expanded to ditch a fixed undercarriage aircraft at night in hurricane seas without a landing light; luckily I have cat's eyes besides nine lives. In a desperate attempt to communicate I got Les Palmer to flash SOS on the cabin lights as we flew alongside.

In the briefing I told Les to recheck the spare engine freight lashings with particular emphasis on stopping the engine joining us in the cockpit with the expected severe deceleration as we hit the water with a fixed undercarriage. Les and Hero put on their lifejackets. I told Les to sit behind the freight in case it moved, and to exit the aircraft from either the side passenger door, or the emergency roof hatch, depending upon whether the aircraft finished up floating on the wings with the cabin full of water or flipped upside down due to the fixed undercarriage. The two up front would exit by the two jettisonable side windows.

I made one pass aiming to put down on the crest of the wave ahead of the boat but we floated so far passed its projected track that I went round again and started earlier.

This time the splashdown was in the right place at the lowest possible speed.

The deceleration was instant; the two cockpit side DV panels were blown in by the weight of water as she settled on the wings. The freight didn't move as I am here to confirm. I cut the magnetos and escaped out of my side, noting that Hero was doing the same. I swam on to the wing. There was no sign of Les, so I released the roof emergency exit. The whole cabin was full of water. Before I could decide whether I was brave enough to dive in and look for Les, a huge wave washed me off the wing. As I went over backwards the crew baggage came spouting out of the hatch like a Roman candle. 'Never mind about the bloody luggage Les,' I mentally shouted. 'Just come out.' With the next big wave Les was also ejected like puppy being born. I swam to Les who was coughing up water and pulled the cord that inflated his life jacket. On impact Les had been thrown forward and had knocked himself out. When he came to he found himself under water. A truly awful moment, but he followed the brief and had found the roof hatch in time to be spewed out by the next wave.

With brilliant seamanship the fishing boat had hove to upwind and was drifting towards us. I started pulling Les in their direction and could see the light on Hero's lifejacket about twenty yards ahead.

I saw Hero being pulled aboard and minutes later we were alongside. Someone threw a rope, which I tied around the recovering Les and he was pulled aboard followed by myself.

On board I quickly established that they were a Spanish fishing boat bound for Cadiz, which we would reach in three days. They confirmed that there were only three of us to pick up. At that point we all watched GAPLN go tail up and slip under the surface. It is hard to judge time at a moment like this, but I estimate she floated for about fifteen minutes. The fishermen said they realized we were in trouble because of the flashing cabin lights and were prepared for something unusual. They were disappointed she sank as they had designs on towing the aircraft to a port and claiming salvage. They then told me that they hadn't really expected to pick up any survivors because two huge sharks had been following the boat for days, feeding off the fish guts they threw overboard as they cleaned up their catch; they thought the sharks would get to us first. I asked them to let some authority know what had happened and that we were all safe. They agreed to try. I think they had an HF communication channel for seafarers. At this point I suddenly remembered that I could not actually speak Spanish and all communication immediately ceased.

I need to make clear that what happened next has got absolutely nothing to do with the ditching. I mention it without comment or explanation because it was what happened next.

For most of my adult life I had had a recurring dream. I was on a boat in rough weather and had just had an unspecified nasty experience that was causing traumatic heavy breathing. In this dream boat I had to sleep in a bunk that was so shallow that I had trouble taking the deep breaths that my agitated state was requiring. This dream was a regular feature of my life and I was always expecting to come across this claustrophobic bunk somewhere in many yachts and small boats of a sailor's interim years. I have already mentioned that in the Navy, ten years before the ditching, when I went for a day trip familiarization in a submarine, as I climbed down the conning tower I clearly remember thinking that this was surely where I was going to find the bunk of my nightmare; but it wasn't there.

When the Spanish realized further communication was impossible because of the language barrier, they showed me to a small narrow cabin, about the size of a walk-in larder. On one wall was a bunk. The co-pilot Hero was already in the top bunk, Les was still coughing up water in the lower bunk and I was invited to lie down on a mattress that was on the deck under the lower bunk. As I laid flat on the floor to wriggle in sideways I realized that I was living my nightmare; that I had already lived this experience many, many times before in my dreams. I was having a pre-cognitive experience that was rubbishing my understanding of logical time. As someone who confidently looks to the scientific for explanations of the mysteries of human existence, I found myself profoundly undermined.

'I dreamed all this before.' I told Les and Hero, but the wary look on their faces warned me that they thought I must be drunk or delirious, and that I'd better never mention this again; so, apart from one or two good looking stewardesses over dinner on nightstops, I never did. I spent the three days of our cruise on the *Exploramar* to Barbate de Cadiz trying to figure out what had happened and what I could have done differently, but I didn't have the necessary facts to come to any firm conclusions. I told Les and Hero that, as was the custom in those days, I would lose my job, but that if they found out about the lifejackets I would lose my licence also. I asked them to be as vague as possible if questioned on this issue and say that all they knew was that they both had a lifejacket each. A few years ago a mutual acquaintance happened upon Les Palmers version of events, which he sent to me and I append it to see if Les tells the same story.

Les Palmer's account

Twin Pioneer G-APLN was to go to Dakar for some route trials with a view to purchase by a French Company called Ardic. Its intended role was to fly between Dakar and The Cape Verde Islands.

It was to be delivered by a British United Airways pilot and I joined it at Southend. We were due to leave on 8th January but we were delayed by radio snags and left on the 9th for Toussus-le-Noble near Paris. The weather was bad and we were diverted to Beauvais. I noticed that the throttle spindle seals on the starboard engine were leaking so I arranged for some new seals to be sent to Toussus-le-Noble.

Captain Williams was in charge and a Captain Costa joined us at Beauvais. We had more problems but managed

73

to get to Toussus-le-Noble and then, because the facilities are much better, onto Le Bourget. This was Friday the 11th, and while the radio was serviced I replaced the throttle seals. I was working single-handed and by the time the radio people had finished it was Monday morning. During the weekend we learned that we had to take on board a Pratt & Whitney engine so on Monday afternoon, I rearranged the seats and got the engine loaded and lashed down.

Captain Costa left us and another French pilot, Mr E. Medina, joined us. With the news that we were to take on still more spares at Casablanca we set off from Le Bourget on the 15th and arrived at Casablanca at about 8.30pm after stops at Biarritz and Seville.

Next morning we loaded what Beechcraft spares we could and set off again in the afternoon for Agadir. It was very rough over the mountains so the skipper decided to land at Marrakech. We got there about 5.30pm.

Three hours 54 minutes to Las Palmas
Refuelling at Marrakech was rough. The airfield is military. The first antiquated bowser was unserviceable and we had to wait for another. Oil was supplied in cans and there was no funnel, so altogether it took some time. I would've liked to have stayed the night but Captain Williams decided to press on and we left at 7:45pm for Las Palmas with a flight plan time of three hours 54 minutes.

It had been very cold over France but it was much warmer here. We were in cloud and the rain was very heavy. I usually had plenty to do on these flights but after about four hours I began to think that we should be getting near Las Palmas. It was dark by now and soon I saw signs of something funny going on. There was a lot of conversation going on between the two pilots though they seemed quite calm.

Captain Williams eventually called me up and told me he was unable to get one of the beacons. Then I heard one of the pilots calling 'Mayday' on the HF and very soon we descended below cloud.

It was still raining heavily. At first, I thought I could see lights but it was just fluorescence. Captain Williams said to look for a light and that he was going to have to make an emergency landing on the water. We were lucky enough to find a ship's light and I was told to signal SOS on the cabin lights and how to do it. We circled the ship several times and the pilot said he was going to ditch. He told us to take off everything except our underclothes and to put on our lifejackets. I opened the top escape hatch and removed the cockpit to cabin door. I suggested a cigarette and Williams remarked that it was a good idea as it might be our last! I strapped myself in the second seat and waited.

In the drink
There was plenty of time to think and plenty to think about. I naturally wondered if the Twin would go right over and whether the P&W engine would come forward at me. Would the props break off and come flying up in my direction? I thought of my family. I prayed. I armed myself with my screwdriver and concentrated on my lap strap release and the lifejacket inflator and light. The impact was very sudden, whether I was knocked out or not I don't know but the next thing I knew was that I was floating near the roof with a mouth full of seawater. During the next few terrifying seconds I managed to feel my way forward and realized I was in the cockpit so I found my way back to the escape hatch. As I emerged, the pilot was on his way back to look for me, apparently he and Medina had left by the side windows that had been forced out by the pressure of water. Williams told me afterwards that he had seen a suitcase appear and thought – surely Les isn't throwing the suitcases out?

Fished out
He checked that we were all OK and said we must stick together but get away from the aircraft. It was raining and

the sea was rough and not too warm. We were about a quarter of a mile from the boat and kept losing sight of it but the crew knew where we were and gradually we made our way to it. It took us about thirty minutes but, at last, we got to within twenty yards, ropes were thrown and we were hauled aboard. Our lifejackets were cut off and we were given warm clothes and put into bunks. I had a fit of the shakes, probably because I heard the crew say that they were surprised they got to us before the fish did. Thank goodness I hadn't realized that there were sharks about or I would have had the shakes even sooner. The coffee wasn't much help but there was nothing stronger to be had.

53 men in a boat

Three days and two nights in a small boat with fifty-three men on board, a rough sea, a diet of fish, beans and potatoes cooked in some crude oil, is not the best treatment for shock but the skipper and his crew were very kind. Captain Williams tried to get him to put in at Agadir but he had to get his fish to Barbate and that's where we arrived on the evening of 19th January.

We were given some more clothing and next day were taken to Gibraltar by road, returning to London by BEA that evening.

Now, continuing my account, the company agent was waiting at Barbate. He took us to a local hotel. We checked in and I went up to my room. No sooner had I closed the door when the phone rang. It was the *Daily Express*. They began a cross examination until I interrupted. I suggested that my chief pilot would be extremely irritated at reading my report of the ditching in the national press before the privilege of interrogating me for himself. I heard later that it was a quiet day for news so all the newspapers had sent their reporters to Heathrow intending to interview me on arrival in Barbate. However, fate intervened again and Hugh Gaitskell, leader of the Labour Party, died. The reporters were all recalled, saving me from my five minutes of fame. Ditching a service-able aircraft might make good news copy, but it is a bummer on a pilot's CV. I have been eternally grateful to the Labour Party ever since. However, a local Kent newspaper reported on 'Basildon man's horrific narrow escape from man-eating sharks.'

The next day we flew home via Gibraltar. Back in London another trauma was to unfold. There would have to be a Court of Inquiry and some interesting facts would emerge. Once again the extraordinary Williams luck would save me from extreme embarrassment.

The Court of Inquiry was held at Gatwick. Because the accident occurred outside UK airspace to a Nigerian registered aircraft and there was no loss of life, the Ministry decided they were not involved, so the adjudicators were all BUA hierarchy. Present were: the Chief Pilot, Chief Navigator, Chief Engineer, Captain Walter Keightley and myself.

I had been encouraged to join BALPA (British Airline Pilots' Association) on the promise of legal representation in the event of an accident. However, this proved a worthless promise. I did not get legal representation; I got Captain Walter Keightley. Walter was a good pilot and thoroughly decent chap, but Perry Mason he was not. I do not recall him saying a word throughout. The most useful legal help I got was a throwaway line by my own solicitor when I went to see him on the matter of the will I should already have written. He said that Courts of Inquiry were different. Whereas in law you were innocent until proved guilty, in an Inquiry you were guilty until you proved your innocence. I wish I had paid more attention to this profound advice because I would have handled my defence differently, maybe even lied a bit if it was necessary.

I was invited to give an account of the events as they had happened, which was effectively a repeat of my report already tendered in writing.

I decided to tell the truth exactly as it happened with the exception of the detail about lifejackets – which was never raised anyway. I was tempted to gild the lily and claim that my radio compass had frozen again, as it had done going into Beauvais two days previously, confirmed in writing in the technical log, but I decided against this principally because it might have obscured what really happened. I really needed to know exactly what had gone wrong with my navigation because my self-esteem was in free fall.

I began proceedings on a light-hearted note saying that they asked me to take a Twin Pioneer to Dakar and sell it. I didn't succeed, but at least I came back with the insurance money. There was no sound in that room except for the thud as my joke fell flat on its face.

There was some general discussion about the accuracy of NDBs and it was established that the Fuerteventura NDB (on request) that I had formally and correctly requested to be switched on between 10 p.m. and midnight in my flight plan had not been switched on at all. To my mind this relieved me of all responsibility for the flight's navigational failings, but then they produced their bombshell.

All flights are required to obtain a weather forecast for their intended route, and it was agreed that the forecast tendered was good and as such that there was no reason not to attempt the flight. What I didn't know was that after an incident involving weather an aftercast is produced by an independent third party. The Gibraltar Met Office produced an aftercast that was virtually identical to the Casablanca forecast. Gibraltar could not find any evidence of any storm at all! It looked as though I was making up the whole storm story as cover for a diabolical error of navigation on my part. I desperately searched around for supporting evidence. What did the Spanish fisherman say? The Board didn't know. What about the reports from Les Palmer and Hero Medina? These confirmed that the sea was a bit rough, but little else. I was in deep trouble!

At this point we adjourned while the Court prepared its firing squad.

In retrospect, it may not be unusual for such a storm as mine to pass unnoticed. Hurricanes, like their cousins, tornados, are very localized. A hurricane may be only a couple of hundred miles wide, while a tornado can be less than ten. I had experienced an intense depression whose size was something in between hurricane and tornado. Any storm moving eastwards in that area would dash itself into extinction on the foothills of the Atlas Mountains on the coast. This region is inhabited only by a few farmers who wouldn't have a phone anyway and no interest in transmitting weather data to Casablanca ATC. My desperate problem was to convince a Court of Inquiry about this.

I was lodged in the *Russ Hill Hotel*, which was the regular crew hotel. I decided to have a beer or three before dinner and in the bar I got talking to a Jersey Airlines co-pilot who was on a Gatwick nightstop. He asked me what I was doing and I told him that I was the notorious pilot of the Twin Pioneer that had ditched off the Canary Islands.

'Oh,' he said. 'We were coming out of Las Palmas that night, the winds were diabolical!'

I might have spilled my beer in my excitement as I clutched this straw of hope and redemption.

'Do you happen to have kept your nav. log?'

'Should be on file back in Jersey,' he said.

The next morning I alerted the Inquiry of my good news and the Board was further postponed until this late evidence was retrieved and considered.

In the end the Board established that the proposed flight was legal, that the aircraft was serviceable, there was sufficient fuel and reserve fuel for the sector, and the weather forecast was suitable. The Board could find no fault in the decisions I became forced to make in the unexpected situation I found myself in. However, the Board decided I was blameworthy for attempting the flight in the first place. Therefore the Board ordered that I should be reduced to the rank of co-pilot for two years.

I was devastated. They could have blamed the Met Office in Casablanca who issued the misleading forecast. They could have blamed the Spanish Aeronautical Control for failing to switch on a properly requested NDB that was critically required for the safe conduct of my flight. But no, I was the captain who had thrown away a perfectly serviceable aircraft, so I was responsible. These were the mores of the day.

Consider Captain Thain of BEA who will always be remembered by the public as the captain responsible for the accident that killed half of Matt Busby's Manchester United team in Munich. However, he will be remembered by pilots as the captain who accidentally discovered the retardant hazards of nose wheel slush; a completely unheard of phenomena since nose wheels were practically a new fangled gadget. Slush can cause an aircraft to stop accelerating on the runway as if it were trying to take off with the brakes on to such a degree that the minimum safe flying speed may never be achieved. Captain Thain had the misfortune to be the first pilot to experience this, but he was still fired out of hand. So, by the mores of the day, I had got off practically scot-free. I suspect my legal aid, the reticent Captain Walter Keightley had been persuasive behind the scenes. I don't know, but it would have been like his style.

I launched an appeal, which was chaired by Freddie Laker. I argued my case all day. By late afternoon Freddie had somehow come to the conclusion that I desperately needed to get to Las Palmas for a tryst with one of the stewardesses arriving there on the West African Safari. He asked me why I was so determined to get to Las Palmas, was I meeting someone? I was so taken aback that all I could think was to say 'Because we hadn't done a day's work yet.' What I should have said was that I wanted to get the HF set frequencies checked overnight by our own resident radio engineer at Las Palmas because the HF was useless, but I doubt it would have made any difference. Freddie was satisfied with his own conclusions and added a third year to my demotion.

Aviation**Safety**Network

an exclusive service of **Flight Safety Foundation** www.flightsafety.org

Accident description

Date:	17 JAN 1963
Type:	Scottish Aviation Twin Pioneer 1
Operator:	Bristow Helicopters
Registration:	G-APLN
C/n / msn:	526
First flight:	1958
Crew:	Fatalities: 0 / Occupants: 3
Passengers:	Fatalities: 0 / Occupants: 0
Total:	Fatalities: 0 / Occupants: 3
Airplane damage:	Written off
Location:	22 km (13.8 mls) off Chepbeica, Morocco (Atlantic Ocean)
Phase:	En route
Nature:	Ferry/positioning
Departure airport:	Marrakech-Menara Airport (RAK/GMMX), Morocco
Destination airport:	Puerto del Rosario Airport, Canary Islands/Fuerteventura Island (FUE/GCFV), Spain

Narrative:
The Twin Pioneer departed Southend on a ferry flight to Dakar. Intermediate night time stops were planned at Marrakech, Agadir, Fuerteventura and Las Palmas. Over Agadir the captain decided to continue to Fuerteventura in the Canary Islands and revised his ETA there. The crew however were not able to contact Fuerteventura by HF or VHF radio. Nor were they able to pick up the Fuerteventura NDB or any other beacon. Uncertain about their position, the captain decided to return to the mainland. Short on fuel, the pilot eventually decided to ditch the plane near fishing vessel.
    It was established that the Fuerteventura NDB was not operating and that the airport had already closed.

EVENTS
ATC & navigation – Navigational beacons inoperative
Result – Emergency, forced landing – Ditching

Sources:
This information is not presented as the Flight Safety Foundation or the Aviation Safety Network's opinion as to the cause of the accident. It is preliminary and is based on the facts as they are known at this time.

[legend] [disclaimer]

copyright 1996 2007 Aviation Safety Network
record last updated: 2005-01-07

(Reproduced courtesy of The Aviation Safety Network)

The above is approximate enough except it makes no mention of the weather, probably because the intense depression was not officially confirmed by either the forecast or the aftercast. It was only supported by the Jersey Airlines crew's navigation log and the backplot, which showed the wind was so strong I only got halfway.

Removing the captain's stripe from my uniform was a disagreeable experience made worse from observing my friends and colleagues trying not to look at the empty scar on my sleeve.

The ditching experience caused a sea-change in my whole attitude to life. Many people have a close brush with the Grim Reaper, are miraculously saved and conclude they were saved for some purpose. I had that doubled and redoubled. The precognitive experience of my recurring dream, for which I could find no rational explanation at the time, was what really kicked my legs out from under. I had looked at the fuel gauges and reckoned I had about an hour left to live and realized that I had not lived the life I would have preferred, and now I never would. Then my course alteration to find the African coast luckily found the eye of the hurricane, and inside the eye I was even luckier to find a fishing boat. A chance was presented, I took it and survived. But I was a different person afterwards. Somebody did die that night and this new person began a career involving much more self-indulgence than I had previously allowed myself. I did what I wanted and the sixties came along with its 'let it all hang out' philosophy – which was a great help.

However, it became the quest of my life to *rationalise* my destabilizing precognitive experience, for which I finally theorized an explanation in my satirical novel. (*Google Sprackenspiel*).

I was to see Les Palmer again ten years later at Prestwick. I was taking a Boeing 707 to Gatwick. We started engines 3 and 4, and while starting number 2, who should be giving me the thumbs up but Les. I considered aborting the engine start to have a nostalgic reunion, but I was already on duty day limits, so sadly I had to let the opportunity go.

I was returned to Southend as a B170 co-pilot. A bonus at Southend was the air hostesses. I have never come across such a collection of beautiful women as happened at Southend – of all places! Flying was still glamorous in those days and the airlines had the pick of the generation. Our girls were literally film star class. We had a Liz Taylor, a Hepburn, a Loren, a Bardot and dozens more who were good looking in their own right. They were in every direction. As a result of which a heavy social scene developed, the best of which were the parties held in a remote barn where we could play all the latest Beatles and Stones records at decibel levels that were a health hazard. The barn was full of bales of hay, alcohol fumes, gyrating bodies and passion. Considering that everybody smoked at that time, it was a marvel the place didn't self-combust.

I served two years of my demotion until Aer Lingus advertised in *Flight* magazine for Boeing 707 co-pilots. This was a chance to leapfrog years of evolution and seniority and get onto the top aeroplane of the day. I was accepted and sent in my resignation. The chief pilot, Jennings, offered me my command back immediately if I would stay; I think I was a little on his conscience. I was flattered, but the Bristol Freighter had no chance when viewed alongside the Boeing 707, and four Calais flights a day looked tired against New York once a week; besides the pay was 40 per cent better than a B170 captain anyway.

Flight magazine was a weekly digest of the aviation scene and for thirty-five years I rarely missed a copy; principally because of the Situations Vacant columns in the back pages. My whole career was shaped by *Flight* magazine's pilots wanted advertisements.

CHAPTER 3

The Airlines: Long Haul

For the first year the job with Aer Lingus was actually as third pilot, a pilot performing the functions of flight engineer. I therefore commenced a very intensive course in the B707 aircraft systems and engineering, which was to serve me well in the future.

Aer Lingus was a delight and Dublin, before the resurgence of the troubles, was one of the most civilized places I have ever lived in. There was a great pub in Howth where you could get a massive steak while listening to the revolutionary songs of 'the troubles' that seemed at the time to be more nostalgic than provocative.

It took some time to get used to the Irish ways. In England, if you got on a bus, you sat as far away from everybody else as was possible. In Dublin, complete strangers would sit next to you and pass the time of day; it was unnerving at first. The most insulting thing you could do in Ireland was to forget somebody's name, so the whole Irish inter-relationship process was intimate and warm.

I had a flat in Dun Laoghaire initially. I used to love coming in from New York at dawn and stopping by the quayside at Dun Laoghaire where the fishermen were unloading their catch. I would buy a huge plaice for two bob for my dinner that evening.

After I qualified on line the flat became an unnecessary expense for just one night per week, so I took lodgings with Maisy McDonagh in Malahide. Maisy was the widow of Irish poet Patrick McDonagh who was an acolyte of the great Yeats. She had two beautiful daughters, the blonde, blue-eyed Caro, and the dark, sultry Boyer. Another pilot colleague also had a room in 1 Church Road, Mike (Flash) Gordon.

Flash was a natural comic and raconteur. I have seen him reduce a restaurant to rubble by impersonating the supercilious hauteur and knock-kneed walk of a pompous New York maître d'. He had a permanent invitation to Mary Quant's dinner table in London's Swinging Sixties scene. I once handed him a feed line he must have been waiting years for.

'Did you ever see *The Guns of Navarone*?'

'See it,' he chortled. 'I am in it.'

Years ago, as a Viking captain, he had been chartered to fly the entire Navarone film crew into and around the Greek Islands as they made one of the best action movies of all time. By the end of the first day, Flash would have been everybody's best friend. Just imagine going down to the local taverna with Gregory Peck, David Niven and Anthony Quinn! He was such a star that the director gave him a job as an extra; as a German trooper, he had to die dramatically, gunned down by Quinn.

I will never forget my first trip to New York. We arrived at dusk and the crew stretched limo took us over the Triboro Bridge. It was a typical mid-west sunset, the sky was blood red and skyscrapers stood out against this as black as vampires. New York was not a bit like Southend-on-Sea, it felt like I was arriving at a foreign planet.

For the Boeing crews, going to New York once every six days meant that you tended to get involved in the local scene. We spent a lot of time in the Village. I saw Erroll

Garner perform live at the Village Gate, which was an unforgettable occasion.

On a check flight, I was in trouble with Aidan Quigley, the chief pilot, for wearing a dirty shirt. In fact, the dirt was rubbing off on my collar from the quick-fit oxygen mask we were obliged to wear continuously around our necks. After I explained this to Aidan he backed off and to mollify me he asked what I was going to do in New York. I told him I intended to see Erroll Garner who was appearing in the Village. He looked a bit puzzled, so I explained 'Erroll Garner, the pianist.'

'Oh', he said. 'I play a bit of piano myself. I'll come with you.'

No matter how well I could play piano, I would never have mentioned it in the same sentence as Erroll Garner, but no matter, off we duly went to the Village. We had to wait ages for the show to begin and Aidan was getting restless because 10 p.m. New York time was 3 a.m. in Dublin. Finally, Garner arrived and began playing in his own unique style. Immediately, our table was knocked over, the beer spilled and Aidan scrambled up.

'I've got to see his hands', he hissed as he shouldered his way forwards to get a better view.

In one tune Garner was playing games with his accompanist by only keying every seventeenth note or so. The base player hung on in there and when they started up perfectly together after some sixteen tortuously lopsided bars, we all erupted with an orgasmic pleasure.

I made friends with Lynda, an American off-Broadway actress whose life seemed to consist of serial rejection as day after day she auditioned trying to break into the big time; there are dozens of actors for every part in New York. I was so impressed by her mental strength and how she managed to stay so positive. Lynda was an English Literature graduate so I brought my early attempts at writing for her to professionally assess at twenty dollars a time – but truthfully I just wanted to be sure she had enough to eat.

Cooking dinner one night in her apartment she sat me down opposite 'so I'm closer to the phone'. She had looks, wit and intelligence, every quality to have made it to the top with a bit of luck, but that phone never rang with the big chance; whereas I met a guy in a bar who claimed he used to be Steve McQueen's flatmate and that one day the phone rang for him, but he was out. So McQueen went instead and the rest is movie history.

Lynda took me to a meeting of the NAACP (National Association for the Advancement of Coloured People). Being Jewish, she had some empathy with the problems minorities were enduring in America, but I didn't realize what was going on. I presumed colour prejudice ended with slavery after the Civil War; after all, 'We hold these truths to be self-evident, that all men are created equal, that they are endowed by their Creator with certain unalienable Rights, that among these are Life, Liberty and the pursuit of Happiness' is a declaration that no self-respecting human could disregard. All the history books insisted that American freedom was what the Civil War was all about. I was unaware how much segregation still existed and completely misunderstood the significance of the event.

At the end, when they stood up to sing 'We shall over-come'. Being implacably anti-religious, I refused to stand. I sat there, the only green-eyed blond in the hall. I was probably lucky to get out without being lynched.

An interesting aside is my chance meeting with an American first class passenger who proudly told me he was retiring home to Ireland after making his fortune. Most unusually I met the same guy a year later on his way back and naturally I asked what went wrong.

'The Irish are all the same,' he complained. 'I missed the Greeks, the Poles, the Mexicans and even the blacks. It got boring.'

The Irish could never be boring. The Aer Lingus crews were typical, both gregarious and talented. John(?) Smith had an impressive bass voice and would sing excerpts from

South Pacific on request in the piano bars that abounded the Village. Dick Quinn used to stand in with The Clancy Brothers who were the most famous recording stars of the Irish revolutionary songs. In the days before INS (Inertial Navigation System – a gyroscopically referenced navigation system that is so accurate it made flight navigators redundant), there were three Ocean Weather Stations positioned at 20, 30 and 40 west (longitude) who would give position fixes and weather reports as we passed overhead. These seamen were holding station for three months in the middle of the wild Atlantic Ocean, so Dick would sing them a song accompanied by his own guitar and mouth organ as we passed overhead. He would put the girls on the radio for a chat so the sailors wouldn't 'get sad'.

The Irish are born entertainers with a natural charm and wit. One day I was waiting for a flight home to Liverpool and sitting next to a guy who was reading the *Irish Times*.

'Would you believe dis?' he exploded. 'Boy wanted for Christmas. So what's wrong with turkey?' We both got sucked into one of those giggling vortexes and nearly missed our flight.

With lockers and showers in the crew room, I found Aer Lingus to be a gentleman's airline and Irish life was sheer civilized pleasure, which makes the resurfacing of the troubles in Belfast ten years later, with all its widows and orphan-making brutality, utterly unfathomable; but I suppose if the Irish were fathomable, they wouldn't be Irish.

My love affair with Ireland began to wane when I read that they proposed to teach mathematics in Gaelic. I thought they were cleverer than that. The function of language in any society is for the purpose of intelligent communication between humans to lessen the risk of misunderstandings leading to quarrels that could otherwise only be resolved by frustrated violence.

The final straw was the blowing up of Nelson's Column in Grafton Street; an unforgivable sacrilege for an ex-Navy man. If it wasn't for Nelson we would all be speaking Napoleonic

French, the Irish included, so when I learned that Cathay Pacific Airways in Hong Kong were looking for experienced jet pilots, I sent in my CV.

Cathay Pacific in Hong Kong and Middle East Airways in Beirut were the two plum jobs for a British licence. Greed may have had something to do with it. As a 707 co-pilot I was earning half as much again as a Bristol Freighter captain and Cathay were offering to double my Aer Lingus take-home pay. I had fallen into a common mantrap by confusing quantity of money with quality of life.

Hong Kong was a strange place in 1967. The mainland Red Guard Chinese were being difficult and had cut off the water supply so water was rationed to four hours' supply every fourth day; it was a time when 'save water, shower with a friend' was coined.

It was the climax of the Red Guard revolution and there were frequent bomb outrages around the city. There was a stunning redhead who was prominently employed at the Ocean Terminal Enquiries Desk in the midst of all the cruise ship shopping outlets. I had arranged to take her out for dinner after my next flight, but when I got back I got a phone call from her father saying she couldn't come because her leg still hurt. I was puzzled. I was familiar with the feminine compulsion to wash hair, but being stood up for a hurting leg was a new one, so I took the hint. It wasn't until months later that I discovered she had been blown up by a bomb placed by her desk, news that wasn't published down route in Tokyo.

I lived in a series of leave flats. Local residents of long standing would go home for three months' leave and preferred someone reliable to house sit. My favourite was on Magazine Gap Road on the saddleback of the Island mountain. On one side I had a balcony that overlooked Kowloon Harbour. The view was vertical and so dazzlingly spectacular that it took me a few days before I could go outside without holding tight onto something. On the other side of the apartment was another spectacular view of Repulse

HM Schoolship Conway

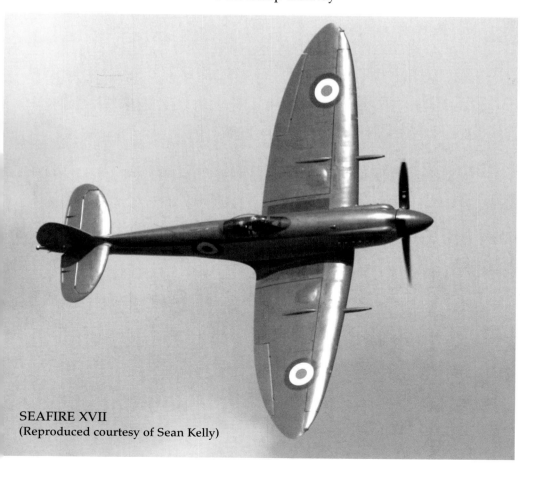

SEAFIRE XVII
(Reproduced courtesy of Sean Kelly)

A Hawker Sea Fury Photograph courtesy of Jenny Coffey (*Airliners.net*)

An Attacker FB11 Photograph courtesy of Joop de Groot (*Airliners.net*)

METEOR 7
by permission of Bill Rich

A Royal Navy Dove or Admirals Barge
Photograph courtesy of Ian Haskell (*Airliners.net*)

THE INSTRUMENT LANDING SYSTEM (ILS) INDICATOR DIAL

Left to regain
Centreline

On the
Centreline

Right to regain
Centreline

Down to Regain
Glideslope

On the
Glideslope

Up to regain
Glideslope

Photograph courtesy of Andrew
Hunt (*Airliners.net*)

Scottish Aviation Twin Pioneer
By permission of Dave Welch

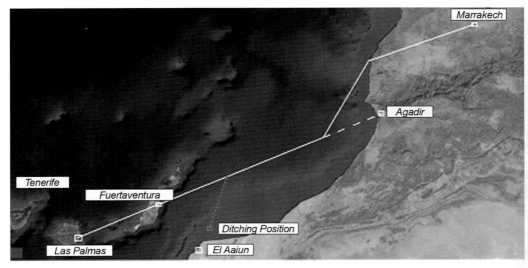

My flight plan and actual track

A British Caledonian 707
Photograph courtesy of Andrew Abshier

A British Caledonian DC10
Photograph courtesy of Paul Robinson (*Airliners.net*)

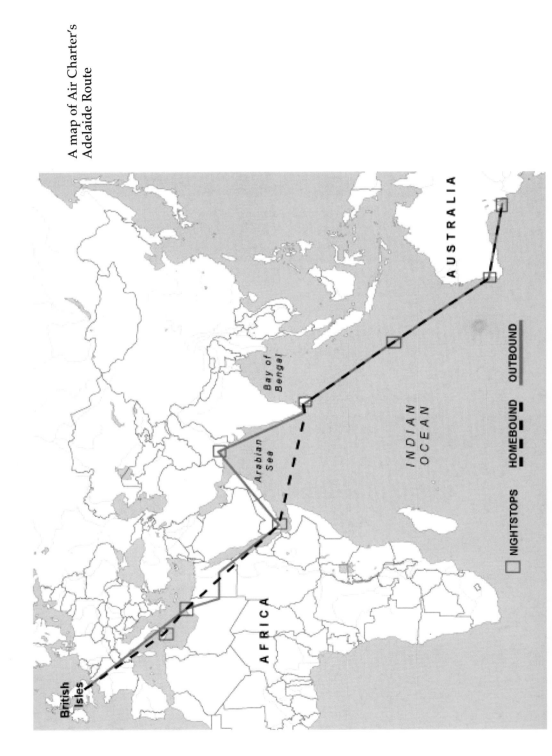

A map of Air Charter's
Adelaide Route

Bay and the beaches. It was the most spectacular place to live until there was a typhoon. I battened down all the steel frame windows, confident that I had done enough, but when the storm hit the noise was terrifying and the rain squeezed through the steel frame windows and arced like a hosepipe onto the carpet in the middle of the room I began to worry. The windows blew out of the apartment on the floor below mine and all the furniture was sucked out into Kowloon Harbour. The family cat was never seen again.

Kowloon was full of young American soldiers on R&R (Rest and Recuperation) from Vietnam. The hotels and girlie bars were making fortunes with round-the-clock riotous parties and frequent fights. I had one sobering conversation in a bar with a young American who looked like James Dean. I was horrified by some of the things he told me; perhaps the most chilling was his admission how much he enjoyed killing.

There were twenty-four of us on the Convair 880 course, twelve pilots and twelve flight engineers. A revealing statistic is that a few years later someone noticed that only one of this twenty-four was still with the wife he arrived with. With amahs to do all the housework, life for the wives could be boring when there was no room in the apartment for any more shopping and there is nothing more dangerous than a bored wife. Paradoxically, for all its exotic Far East glamour, Hong Kong could be very claustrophobic. The chaps got away to Tokyo and Singapore but the wives were locked in for eighteen months and divorce is an easy option when you can comfortably afford it.

After the Aer Lingus 707s the Convair 880 was a bit primitive. For example, the pressurization was inclined to fill the cabin full of oil fume smoke and many of the systems were idiosyncratic and not as refined as later became standard.

I found Cathay Pacific had a lot of unique ideas. The conversion course for the Convair 880 consisted of a training engineer reading the entire training manual out loud in the classroom, end to end and word for word. I was more used to getting on with such tasks by myself and in my own time. In retrospect, I think the reasoning behind this method was so that you could never say 'I didn't know that' because the response would always be 'it was read out to you'. I found the method a difficult way to learn.

'Training' was evolving into the emergent safety philosophy in the airlines, and I was at fault initially to resist this trend. Where were the trainers when I really needed them; when I did my first solo in Spitfires; when I was struggling to pass my Instrument Rating? If I got myself into a mess I was used to sorting myself out. My operating philosophy was already well defined; I tried to correct my mistakes before they happened.

There is a world of difference between being 'checked out' and being 'trained'. When you were 'checked out', another captain sat in and checked that your techniques were safe and practical; the recognized measure of competence was that the trainer would be happy to send his wife and kids with you. Being 'trained' meant you did not get checked out until you had learned to fly in a precise way, the same way as everybody else. I resented this intrusion into my natural flair and being turned into some kind of cockpit monkey. I was a bit of a pain in the arse. Having admitted that, I wasn't entirely in the wrong.

As an oversimplification, there evolved two types of training captains who had to deal with two types of pilot. Pilots who find the job easy take developments in their stride and do not need a deal of training. Pilots who find the job stressful have to work hard at it. For natural pilots the job is about flair, for the rest the job is about numbers. The latter tend to learn what to do methodically and mechanically. These same two polarizations also apply to training captains. Some trainers have a flair for it and some seem to need the power and have more in common with the Gestapo. In the real world all pilots, and training captains, fall somewhere within these polarizations. Trainers who see themselves as the policemen of the airline should not be let anywhere near an aircraft in an official capacity.

Digressing a little on the subject of 'trainers', British Caledonian Airways was blessed with many good trainers. One of the best was Graham Kneath.

After ten years on the Boeing 707, continually on the move like the Flying Dutchman, for ever adjusting to time zone changes, my sleep patterns became irregular and I was suddenly very tired. The long all-night sectors had also strained my eyes and I was having to get used to wearing spectacles, which, oddly enough, was one of the hardest problems I ever had to deal with in flying. I hated having to adjust my instinctive technique to cope with this emergent disability. I desperately needed a break so I bid for the short-haul BAC 1-11 fleet for a rest and more normal hours.

Graham Kneath was our rostered trainer. Why I say *our* is because my co-pilot was also under training because he was trying to get his licence back after having been dried out. I had known this co-pilot since Southend and he was more than worth salvaging.

We were in the BA simulator at Heathrow practising various take-off engine failures before and after minimum safety speed. My co-pilot was obviously rusty and was having problems with his short-term memory retention. He kept forgetting that on a reduced thrust take-off (a procedure for engine conservation by only using as much power as you need for take-off), the first thing you do if you lose an engine is to apply full power on the remaining good engine.

Graham managed him like a stand-up comic working an audience. We did nothing except take-off engine failures, and whenever he forgot the power it was a joke, and when he forgot again it was funnier and then it became hilarious. For two hours we did nothing else but runway work and Graham never uttered a word nor even a nuance of criticism that might undermine our co-pilot's fragile convalescent confidence. By the end of the detail my co-pilot was very tired, but it was all coming back to him.

Contrast this with my own experience six months later on my first BAC 1-11 base check. The check was on a normal scheduled Manchester flight. We were running late so I was moving things along a bit, such as instead of cruising at the company maximum fuel economy speed, I deliberately added 20 knots. If anything was said at the time, I do not recall, but when we got back to Gatwick the training captain said I had failed my check. He had a support page full of defects that I would classify as mostly idiosyncratic or trivial; I still have this document. For example, the wheels were actually moving before I switched on the anti-collision light. He may have been correct, but it was no more than the first yard. He snagged me for the next three trips under supervision with other training captains.

I don't know if you've ever been unexpectedly punched in the stomach by Mohammed Ali, but that is what it felt like. I was shattered because it was such utter rubbish, but what was worse was that I was suddenly drained of all self-confidence. Those three under supervision sectors were a nightmare. I was literally on the point of mental breakdown and couldn't even remember a QNH (an altimeter pressure reference) unless I had written it down. I just hung on in there in a state of panic. Luckily my next three sectors were with more talented trainers and I slowly repaired, but I was never the same pilot afterwards; something had been cauterized and only scar tissue remained. I had to fly exactly by the book and had been transformed into a cockpit monkey.

I have kept all my check reports, so perhaps the value of this training captain's comments should be weighed against the thirty-five others covering the ten previous and ten subsequent years, which were all either 'Satisfactory' or 'Very Satisfactory' with a couple of 'Above Average'. I can only conclude that there was a hidden agenda at work here, but I don't know what this was or why. All I know is that this guy very nearly destroyed me, and that is the antithesis of what a good trainer should be. It has famously been said

94

that those who can, do, those who can't, teach. Maybe I had it coming, maybe I was insufficiently deferential, all I know is it was an extremely untalented way to handle any pilot.

A very dear friend was a Cathay Pacific training captain. One summer we dog-sat for him in his French Mas while he and his wife took a long waltz around Australia. He left explicit instructions on how to manage the property. His swimming pool instructions began with the words 'Go to pool', which goes some way to explaining the training captain mentality. They are inclined to assume that everybody else is stupid, not clever like them.

This digression in time background leaves us suitably briefed to consider how I came to leave Cathay Pacific.

I was the rostered co-pilot on the Convair 880 while another co-pilot, Stan McPhee, was under command checks. The training captain was the famous Laurie King. Laurie King was a numbers pilot; one who believed there was a precise time to perform a precise event in a precise sequence, a technique that must have saved Laurie King and he was rigidly imposing his salvation upon the airline. Would-be captains with natural flair would grit their teeth and comply until they were checked out, then go back to normal. It's reasonable to say that if you survived a Cathay Pacific command course you were a thick-skinned pilot of above average skill.

Unfortunately, King's training philosophy was not in line with my own. In no time he was ignoring the captain under training and was concentrating on me. Almost everybody smoked in those days, and King was insisting I should hold my cigarette in my left hand to free up my right hand to hold my pencil and attend to the nav. log, unless I was left-handed. I should pick up my microphone with my non-writing hand so that my writing hand was free to copy ATC instructions. While his comments were no more than common sense they were not an industry mandate. In the end I was getting flustered and in frustration I pointed out to him that I was the legal qualified co-pilot attempting to perform the functions of my licence, and he was bugging me to distraction. He ordered me out of the cockpit and filed a check report criticising me as being 'untrainable'.

So ended my Cathay Pacific career. I was invited to meet with the general manager and discuss the issues but I realized that, with somebody like Laurie King, I would never get a command in Cathay, so I resigned. I probably could have smoothed things over if I had tried, but frankly, though I enjoyed Hong Kong and admired the airline, it was all happening back in swinging London and I couldn't wait to get home. With hindsight I was also probably a bit lonely as my wife had not joined me in Hong Kong, having enrolled on a course of training to be a teacher. The truth is that she was an early feminist and I was a late chauvinist, so we were diverging and subsequently divorced.

Cathay gave me three months in lieu of notice and a ticket to London via San Francisco, where I wanted to call in on IASCO, a recruitment agency, who were looking for pilots for various airline contracts. It turned out that IASCO were only looking for experienced jet captains. I spent a few days with Lesley Hall from Southend and her new husband Michael Rosenberg who was bravely publishing new poetry. 'If You're Going to San Francisco' was at the top of the charts and I was right there. Flower Power had just arrived in the Haight Astbury, which was full of people colourfully demonstrating their individuality by all wearing blue trousers called jeans, sitting in trees smoking something exotic and observing how everything was 'cool man, cool'. I continued eastwards back home to Liverpool, which was temporarily the capital of the pop world.

The only interesting job to be found in the ubiquitous *Flight* magazine was a job as a pilot of a private jet for Tiny Rowlands (chairman of the Rio Tinto Zinc Corporation). There was to be a lot of European flying, but the principal task was flying Tiny to Salisbury in Southern Rhodesia, nowadays called Harare in Zimbabwe. I did the Fanjet Falcon course at Dassault's factory in Bordeaux and was in the middle of a checkout flying around Europe when Ian Smith declared UDI (Unilateral Declaration of Independence) and Rhodesia became out of bounds.

Tiny was very apologetic. He would have to put the aircraft on the Swiss register and hire a couple of German pilots to fly it. He said I would get three months' pay in lieu of notice. I suggested six, to which he readily agreed. I was having my best year ever; it was June and already I had been paid for eleven months having only worked for two.

I had always liked the look of Caledonian Airways, which later became British Caledonian Airways following the merger with British United Airways. Their owner, Adam Thomson, was an ex-Fleet Air Arm pilot who had steadily built up his airline from scratch and had just purchased two Boeing 707s.

Since I already had the Boeing 707 on my licence Caledonian Airways were pleased to see me. They were expanding so fast that by the end of one year they had three more Boeings and I found myself on a command course. To get a command on a four-engine jet with just one year's seniority is unique in a seniority ridden industry.

British Caledonian took up twenty years of my life that I wouldn't swap with a Beatle, and the first ten years as a Boeing captain, tramping around the world, rarely going to the same place twice, with four overstretched chaps up the front and seven over-excited girls down the back was even better than that. Just picking a month at random from my log book, I note I had stopovers in Manila, Karachi, Bangkok, Hong Kong, Sydney, Melbourne, Honolulu, San Francisco, Bermuda, Tenerife, Nairobi, Lusaka and Boston. Seven of those airfields I had never seen before, so you had to be really sharp. If heaven is anything like as good as those ten years, I will accept an invitation to relocate.

I was checked out by John Ryder. Unlike Cathay Pacific, there was no rigid mandatory operating technique. You flew it as you saw fit, and the check captain would sit in and either approve or disapprove of your technique. John must have liked my style, which was basically a modified Aer Lingus system, and I was checked out. I knew I had passed because of an incident going into Prestwick.

From Toronto, we were positioning for a straight-in landing to the east when the control tower called a wind change and told us to call downwind for a landing to the west. This we did, but on the approach suddenly the most extreme turbulence broke out. I was fighting with the controls to stay roughly on the ILS (Instrument Landing System) and curiously I couldn't keep the speed down. We were uncontrollably about 40 knots above the recommended approach speed, Vref, with the thrust levers at idle. I was just about to throw it away and overshoot when it just as suddenly stopped and the air became smooth as gin. I added thrust to meet the falling airspeed and we landed normally and smoothly, a real greaser. As we taxied in the cockpit door burst open and the chief steward stormed in. 'What the fuck happened there?' he demanded angrily. 'I thought we were going to crash.'

'I don't know,' I admitted, 'I've never known turbulence quite like that. I was just about to go around again when it stopped.'

'What are you talking about?' John asked. 'I didn't notice anything.'

So we told him.

'Well I didn't feel a thing,' John repeated, and I knew I was checked out.

I still don't know exactly what happened to the air mass on that approach. My best guess is that the wind change caused the air to roll, like a breaker crashing up a beach and we found ourselves freewheeling down the roll like a surfer.

My first trip in command was a Las Palmas freighter to bring back tomatoes. By a strange coincidence we passed very close to the position where I had ditched the Twin Pioneer and lost my command almost seven years to the day previously.

Because of my Cathay Pacific time, I was considered the Hong Kong expert and my next trip was to Hong Kong with a freighter. Part of the freight was a dog in a kennel destined for Cathay Pacific's chief pilot. On the tarmac in Hong Kong, Captain D. Smith duly arrived to pick up his dog and he thanked me for looking after it.

'You don't remember me,' I said, standing there, the captain of a shiny new Boeing 707; bigger and more beautiful than Cathay's old second-hand Convair 880s. 'You sacked me a year ago because Laurie King said I was an untrainable co-pilot.'

It was a moment to treasure.

Besides unusual air mass movements such as that on the Prestwick landing, fog, fire, thunderstorms and structural failure, are the other spectres of a pilot's recurring night-mares. Of these, structural failure, such as a wing falling off, is the worst. You can't do anything about structural failure except write a quick will. I have never experienced a structural failure, as I am here to demonstrate, but I did get very close from an airborne engine fire.

We, an entire BCAL Boeing 707 crew, were positioning to Singapore on BA (British Airways) in one of their Rolls-Royce Conway-engined Boeing 707s.

As we rotated at take-off I heard a noise like a champagne cork being pulled, then the sky outside my window turned red and yellow with streaks of silver as number one engine exploded and caught fire. The noise that 180 passengers make when they think they are all going to die is indescribable; you have to be there. My own contribution to this banshee wail was something like 'Oh no, not as a bloody passenger!' Looking out of my window, I could see the fire. I could understand the reddish yellow colour was burning fuel, but what worried me were the strong streaks of silver that could only be coming from melting metal. It was not looking good. Mo Sparham, my flight engineer, was sitting next to me, and he said, 'Ron, I think I'll go and sit down the back.' I understood his thinking; passengers sitting in the rear of an aircraft have, statistically, a better chance of survival, albeit no better than one per cent. It seemed like a good idea at the time, so we both got up and relocated to the rear. It was such a stupid, thoughtless thing to do that I cringe even now at the recollection. We could have caused a panic, and if every passenger on that aeroplane had followed our example, the shift in weight could have caused our desperate captain in the cockpit extra control problems he didn't need at this moment in time.

The aircraft turned back for an immediate landing, and at some point on the downwind leg the fire went out. We landed normally and were bussed back to the passenger terminal.

I learned through the pilot's grapevine what had happened in the cockpit. You cannot see the rear of any of the engines from the cockpit of a Boeing 707, so the pilots were not aware they were on fire; they were only aware that they had had an engine failure. When the compressor disintegrated it had shed blades all over the inside of the cowling. These compressor blades, which had been rotating at something like 12,000 revolutions per minute, caused massive secondary damage. Some had severed the fire warning system, so the pilots had no indication that they had an engine fire. Others had severed the fire extinguishing pipes, so the pilots could not have put out the fire they didn't know they had. Like professionals they went through the drills and shut down the engine, closing the fuel cut-off cock in the process. This duly isolated the engine from the normal fuel supply. However, the compressor blades had also severed the fuel lines before the shut-off valve, so the fire was still being fed directly from the fuel tanks in the wing. On the downwind leg, our ace flight engineer in the cockpit, this beaut of a guy who will never buy another drink in his life while I am in the bar, had continued with the secondary items in the check list and closed the tank valve. Shortly thereafter, now

100

starved of fuel, the fire went out. The significance of this act was that at flying speed a fire behaves like a welding torch, and the silver streaks in the flames that I mentioned were the wing spar being melted by the blowtorch heat. It was calculated that this spar would have lasted for about thirty more seconds before structural failure, which would have led to outer wing detachment and a catastrophic crash fatal to us all.

The principal dangers of thunderstorms are lightning, hail and turbulence. Theoretically, aircraft are designed to cope with lightning strikes. Safety is achieved by electrically bonding every single unit of an aircraft's construction so that no gaps are left. When lightning strikes an aircraft, hundreds of thousands of volts and amps are looking for a way to earth. Since an aircraft isn't connected to earth, somehow lightning generally realizes it is wasting its time. However, if the constructional bonding is not complete, this might leave a gap between two pieces of metal. Should lightning strike in this case, hundreds and thousands of volts and amps will find the gap and arc across it in much the same way as the sparking plug in a car engine. Not necessarily a fatal experience, but if that gap happens to be in your fuel tank, it is unlikely that you would have enough time to regret this.

The next danger is hail. All hail falls from thunderstorms. In some parts of the world hail the size of tennis balls have been recorded. It doesn't require much imagination to visualize the dangers of flying at five hundred miles an hour through a cloud of suspended pieces of ice the size of tennis balls. I saw a Boeing 707 at Boston that had just flown through a hail storm. Every leading edge was a mass of dents and both cockpit windows were crazed; it was due for a major rebuild.

Finally, turbulence: those tennis ball-sized hailstones are not suspended in space by some kind of levitation trick. They are held in the air by vertical columns of air going upwards, so as you can imagine, it takes quite a strong upwards gust to hold up a cloud of tennis ball-sized chunks of ice. What goes up must come down, so alongside these vertical up currents are vertical down currents. Besides the difficulty of steering an aircraft through such a maelstrom, it was soon realized that these currents of air were strong enough to cause wing loads in excess of the designed limitations leading to structural damage with the obvious dire results. A further feature of downdraughts is that they can be extremely dangerous when the aircraft is on the approach and close to the ground. A downdraught can be so strong as to completely misalign the airflow over the wing and nullify its lift causing a stall. Being low on the approach also precludes the ability of recovering from a stall because you haven't the available height to push the nose down to recover the lost airspeed. Aircraft have been known to have been stalled into the ground a mile or so short of the runway. Today this phenomenon is well understood and all kinds of drills, simulator exercises, monitoring and warning devices are employed to warn the pilots. The first thing any pilot learns about thunderstorms is to stay well away from them.

Actually, that's not quite correct. A thunderstorm itself may be a danger to navigation, but it's an incredibly localized phenomena. You can fly a few yards from a thunderstorm in the smoothest air you could ever hope to find. I used to fly close by thunderstorms to let bored passengers be in awe at its purple and violet convulsing majesty. I say 'used to' because I was coming out of Houston one night and saw a thunderstorm that was flashing lightning sideways. I had always presumed that lightning was an air to ground event, but this MF was convulsing sideways. I immediately adjusted my thunderstorm fly by technique to twenty miles.

In the days before weather radar we often had to delay until a thunderstorm danger had passed. If we were caught in a thunderstorm in the DC4 fleet we just had to close our eyes and trust to luck. Some captains would descend to the lowest safe altitude because, at least, that avoided the extremes of turbulence although it increased the risk of hail. Nowadays we have fantastic equipment that shows us exactly where the storm cells are, and the echo is colour coded so that we can see where the strongest turbulence is likely to be.

Weather radar is always fitted in the nose cone. Its advantages have to be balanced by the fact that its transmissions induce thunderstorms to respond, so these days, the majority of lightning strikes are on the nose of the aircraft. I have seen filmed proof that lightning strikes can be induced. The film showed rockets being fired up under thunderstorms, which were immediately followed by a downwards lightning strike, so there is a slight tendency for weather radar transmissions to induce a return strike, but it is rare. Generally, a thunderstorm recognizes that a properly bonded aircraft has no usable connection to earth and so is a waste of its time to mess around with it.

It also takes some sangfroid for pilots to adjust to the fact that there are strong microwave transmissions going on in between your legs. In fact, the weather radar doesn't rotate like most radar aerials, it oscillates, so that the radiation is never aimed backwards, and the cockpit is shielded anyway, but worry isn't always logical.

One of the oddest manifestations of thunderstorm activity in the aircraft can be seen on the cockpit windscreen. The strong static activity often causes arcing sparks that leap about the windscreen like will-o'-the-wisps and often causes panic in those not prepared for it. Many a crew meal tray has been abandoned in mid-air by a rapidly retreating rookie stewardess.

Aircraft have been struck by lightning many times without incident, and curiously rarely causing any damage. There is one famous account of a strike where a ball of something, probably negative electrons, appeared in the cockpit, passed through the closed cockpit door as if it wasn't there, and rolled down the aisle, crumpling an empty beer can that had been carelessly abandoned on the floor. It then disappeared out of the tail of the aircraft leaving behind 180 dumbstruck passengers all doubting the evidence of their eyes and just grateful to be still alive.

My own most interesting strike was coming out of Gatwick in a DC10. As we turned northwards towards our transatlantic entry point I happened to be looking eastwards and saw the strike come in horizontally like an incoming missile. It hit number three engine cowling a mighty blow that sounded like an explosion. We continued as cleared and began to look around for signs of damage. The only sign of any problem was that number three EGT gauge (exhaust gas temperature) was at zero, although the engine itself was operating normally. We continued the climb as cleared while we discussed the significance of this strike. The chief stewardess came into the cockpit and begged me to say something on the PA (Passenger Address) as the passengers were in a ferment.

I decided that we could not safely proceed to Los Angeles, crossing thousands of miles of polar winter landscape without a serviceable EGT gauge, which is the primary instrument for measuring the health and efficiency of an engine, so we told air traffic control that we needed to return to Gatwick and dump all our fuel on the way. I hate dumping tons of expensive fuel over southern England.

I told the passengers what had happened and that, although we still had three good engines, we had decided it was wiser to go back to Gatwick. I believe they thought so too.

On the way back the flight engineer said he thought he could detect a drop in number three fuel pressure that could indicate a leak, so I decided, as a precaution, we would shut down number three engine on the approach, which would give it time to cool down in the airflow so as to be too cool to ignite any fuel that might possibly be sloshing around in the cowling. Everything went to plan, and we taxied back to the stand followed by the fire tenders.

104

The significance of this story is that when we examined the number three engine cowling, all we could see was a tiny entrance hole the size of a pinprick. Through this tiny hole, the lightning had entered the cowling and struck the EGT gauge a mighty blow enough to render it useless. I repeat, the first thing a pilot learns about thunderstorms is to have absolutely nothing to do with them except to genuflect from a safe distance.

The above are the exterior menaces to aircraft safety, but there are interior ones. Flying with two captains is notoriously risky.

Flying a modern jet is a two-person job because there is too much to do for one person to be operating at maximum safety. What has evolved is something similar to marriage where one person deals with the outside world, and the partner deals with the house. The captain concerns himself with the outside environment. Are there any thunderstorms ahead? What shall I do if the destination airfield becomes unusable due to weather or runway blockage? Meanwhile, the co-pilot will ensure that all the radio position reports are made and that the fuel and air-conditioning systems are operating correctly. With two captains in the front there is the danger that both captains are concerned with the outside environment and nobody is keeping an eye on the interior situation. A typical example of the danger of this is during the final part of a bad weather instrument approach. With both pilots straining to locate the weather-obscured runway ahead there is nobody to point out that the rate of 800 feet a minute to 1,500 feet a minute, a mere slight reduction of back pressure on the control column, but if you are only at 300 feet above the ground when it happens the aircraft is only seconds away from disaster. A good co-pilot would never have allowed such a slip to develop.

One night in Toronto when the passengers were boarding, the cockpit door was open and most of the passengers were peering inside as they passed by. One passenger passed and then turned back saying, 'Harry is that you?'

It turned out that he recognized my flight engineer and together they had survived a tour of operations in Lancaster bombers in the Second World War.

Later on in the cruise, knowing about the appalling loses endured by the bomber crews when 55,573 aircrew were lost (44.4 per cent), I asked Harry which was the worst. Were the night-fighters the most deadly or was it the anti-aircraft fire?

'Frankly,' he said, 'our stupidity and lack of experience was as big a danger as the other two. There were a lot of collisions in the massed raids due to somebody flying at the wrong height, a lot of crews got lost, ran out of fuel or into high ground, some even were hit by our own bombs dropped from above because they arrived over the target too early or too late.'

Some pilots are never off the PA (Passenger Address), but I was never comfortable with this method of communication. My habit with passengers was to always tell the truth and I did make one or two interesting calls.

We were on a series of charters to Singapore, and the airways route invariably passed overhead Turin. At the time I was driving a Fiat 850 that I had shipped home from Hong Kong. This car was more pretty than reliable, so as we passed over Turin I used to announce 'Ladies and gentlemen, this is your captain speaking, we are now passing over Turin, the home of the Fiat motor car company. I've got a Fiat car, and if I had it with me I'd drop it on them.'

On another occasion I said 'Ladies and gentlemen, you may be wondering why we are taxying out with an estimated arrival time at Houston that is exactly the same as Hurricane Gilbert. So let me explain. Plan A is to go to Houston because the paths of hurricanes aren't always predictable. Plan B is to go to Dallas. Just in case neither option looks good, I've got enough fuel on board to take us to Rio de Janeiro. So sit back and relax and I'll keep you updated as I become aware of any significant developments myself.' On the day,

106

Hurricane Gilbert veered away and we landed without a problem at Houston.

On another flight full of boy scouts going to a jamboree in Canada, I was trying to describe our polar Great Circle routeing to the group who were following through on the Mercator map in the company magazine. As I pointed out the various waypoints along the route, I had to admit 'It obviously looks like a huge unnecessary curve into the frozen north. But it isn't. In fact it's a straight line. This is not your lucky day, chaps; you are flying with the pilot who is telling you the map is wrong.'

In its charter years Caledonian Airways often flew the Hadj. This was a contract to fly the Faithful from Islamic centres such as Tripoli and Benghazi to Jeddah for the annual religious festival at Mecca; this was a massive logistical nightmare as millions of Muslims arrived from all over the world. Most of our passengers were dirt-poor farmers whose trip to Mecca had been paid for by the local oil-rich sheikh. We were briefed about not touching food with the left hand. The girls were puzzled by the discovery that the toilet seats all had footmarks on them until we realized that our passengers had never seen a toilet seat before, and preferred to squat over the hole in the traditional way. This information was to spawn a line of reasoning that we will revisit later.

For the crews it was an opportunity to hunt for bargains in the souk. Gold was cheap because it was sold strictly by weight with little extra charge for necklace and ring craftwork.

Alcohol was strictly forbidden but some of the crews found a supplier of Sediki, an illicit, locally distilled bootleg spirit of dubious quality and safety. We had several professional drinkers in the airline so we sent them in ahead and monitored their condition. When they were still alive the next morning we all joined in the party. The local Arabs were very hospitable and used to take the crews to the

Creek, a swimming beach about twenty miles up the coast. Camels had only recently been replaced by Cadillacs, but even so, every five miles or so the convoy would stop and check that there were no thorns in the Cadillac's tyres. The Arabs would bring a live lamb for the evening barbeque and it would be slaughtered (throat cut) halal-style, and hung for bloodletting. The girls were invariably scandalized and nothing would induce them to eat that cruelly abused lamb. However, as the sultry night descended and the smell of the barbeque spit pervaded the night air, I noticed that they tended to drift back in and allow themselves to be persuaded to try a little.

One night we were invited to one of the prince's palaces for a cocktail party. For diplomatic purposes, there was no shortage of spirits here and the crews fell upon this diplomacy like dehydrated legionnaires happening on an oasis. At one stage I distinctly recall looking at a gin and tonic and noticing, for the first time, how beautiful it was in the candlelight; pretty bubbles gleaming like miniature diamonds. I mentioned this odd experience to our steward the next morning.

'That was the candles,' he informed me with worldly condescension. 'They were spiked with marijuana.' If it was true I can record that this single isolated 'trip' did not turn me into an addict as it remains my only experience of drugs except for alcohol, tobacco, Alka-Seltzer and aspirin.

One of the great strengths of Caledonian was that the accounts department knew on Monday morning how well the company had performed the previous week. A feature of this was the Captain's Account.

In Caledonian Airways, the captain was a captain in every sense of the word. He had to be ready for anything. I carried a stack of tickets in case a last-minute passenger charter should occur down route. I wrote a ticket for my girlfriend and took her with me to Hong Kong on a seven-day Christmas slip.

Prior to any trip, a captain would, from experience, advise the cashiers how much money he needed to pay for the proposed trip. This would be drawn in sterling and/or dollars traveller's cheques and the captain would be responsible for paying the landing fees to the airport authorities, handling charges, payable to the company agents, hotel bills and the crew allowances. Fuel was the only charge that was on credit. On return to base the captain would file his account of the total flight costs. By simple arithmetic the accounts department would know exactly where the profit and loss balance stood almost at any moment in time. This permitted instant adjustments of business tactics as the circumstances unfolded.

The only time in my life when I have been awash with money was during a series of charters to the Far East. I had to pay for the crew hotel, the landing fees and the agent's handling charges in local currency, which I was obliged to account for at the official rate of exchange. However, we were all besieged by moneylenders who were offering local currency for dollars at twice the official rate so I was trousering wallets of profit. A Cally captain was an entrepreneur; more like a ship's captain in the days of sail. Many brought in new business; one was so successful he bought himself a yacht from the profits.

That seven-day Christmas slip in Hong Kong when I took my girlfriend spawned another story. All the girls were very excited to get in amongst all that bargain shopping, and there were tears when I got a signal from crewing changing their minds, and that we should position home leaving on Christmas Eve, arriving home on Christmas morning.

'Fine,' I said, over the phone, 'the shops will be shut so get your pencil ready, I want you to buy me a ten-pound turkey, three bottles of wine, some Christmas crackers, a pudding and a bag of mixed nuts. Have you got all that?' I asked.

'Yes, I got all that,' he replied.

'Now the first officer wants a fifteen-pound turkey, six bottles of wine, some Christmas crackers ...'

'Okay, okay,' the person on the phone said. 'I get the message. Stay where you are and come back as rostered.'

Not only had I brought my girlfriend, but the engineer's girlfriend had flown in from Singapore for a reunion.

We had a great time, with parties every night with my friends from Cathay Pacific who lent us cars so we could explore. A trip to Portuguese Macao was arranged, and then cancelled at the high-speed ferry gangway because half the party forgot to bring their passports.

On 30 December we took off to come home. The engineer's girlfriend was left behind in tears.

We were in the climb out when Hong Kong called us and said there had been a bomb threat and that we had to return to the colony.

I looked across at the engineer and raised my eyebrows in a question.

'No,' he confirmed confidently. 'She wouldn't do a thing like that'.

So we dumped forty tons of fuel and landed back.

The Hong Kong police were very aggressive and disagreeable with us as well as the passengers as they searched the aircraft and our luggage. This should not be so unexpected when you recall that a Cathay Pacific jet had been blown up by a bomb placed in his wife's suitcase by a Bangkok police inspector. Naturally, he had taken the precaution of insuring her life for several hundred thousand pounds in one of those automatic machines that used to be found in all major airports. We went back to the hotel where the flight engineer's girlfriend was waiting. Many years later he told me that she had owned up, not realizing how serious it was.

As an aside, I heard a rumour, also probably apocryphal, that the Cathay Pacific crews had clubbed together and taken out a contract on that Thai police inspector should he ever get out of prison.

Shortly after this Caledonian Airlines merged with British United Airways to become British Caledonian Airlines

(BCAL) and I was reunited with many old friends from BUA and the Channel Airbridge.

British Airways were considering buying out BUA, who were struggling because their allowed route structure was insufficient to support a quality scheduled airline, and BA had, I believe, made an offer. If accepted this would make BA a colossal monopoly, which the Government did not consider would be in the best interests of the travelling public. Caledonian was a charter company expanding exponentially and some bright person floated the idea that, if Caledonian merged with BUA to form an effective competition to BA, the Government would award the newly merged airline with some choice revenue-earning routes that would make it a viable competitor.

Adam Thomson raised the capital and the deal went through, but the merger caused a few headaches principally, for pilots, in the area of seniority. Seniority is no small issue in the airline industry. In most established airlines, promotion comes as a function of seniority and seniority commences from a pilot's date of joining. There are variations to this rule of thumb, but generally speaking it resolves a lot of squabbles if every pilot gets a chance of a command in seniority order. The problem between BUA and Caledonian was that BUA was a much older company and twice the size of Caledonian. If the seniority list was merged on the basis of date of joining, then most Caledonian captains would find themselves junior to most BUA co-pilots, i.e. Boeing 707 captains would find themselves junior to BAC 1-11 co-pilots; theoretically, the 707 captains should be demoted and re-trained on the 1-11, and vice versa.

Besides the command issue, seniority can also influence the monthly pay check. In most of the large companies, rostering for a whole month of flights would be broken down into the most efficient lines of work for an individual pilot. Then these lines of work would be offered to the pilots to choose their preference, which was then awarded in seniority order, the senior pilots getting the most agreeable work schedules and the junior pilots getting the weeks on standby and any other rubbish. Because flying is such a non-routine lifestyle, a pilot could use his seniority to bid for those flights that fitted his wife's hopes for some normal home life or the line of work that accrued the greatest fringe benefits, i.e. overtime and allowances. Rough justice, but since bidline was seniority based, everybody would achieve the benefits as they became more senior themselves.

For reasons beyond comprehension, Caledonian's Chairman of the Pilot's Association, Tony Stickland, was prepared to accept a merged seniority list based on the date of joining, but it was clearly a cost non-runner in an airline that was cash-strapped as a way of life. Even if the status quo were permitted to maintain, I was not disposed to quietly surrendering all the proposed benefits of the merger, the transfer of scheduled services from BA, to fellow pilots merely because they had joined their own company earlier than I had joined mine. I wrote an impassioned protest and pinned it on the Pilot's Notice Board requesting all pilots who felt as I did, should contact me to consider some concerted action. This potential tsunami of reaction was picked up by Adam Thomson and I was called into the office to expand my views. Adam wisely nipped this divisive disagreement in the bud unilaterally imposing the solution I had suggested, the two lists would be merged from the top. The first name would be Caledonian's number one followed by BUA's number one and two, and so on. In consideration that nothing causes more trauma amongst pilots than seniority squabbles, this solution was Solomonic, everybody stayed more or less where they were so the benefits offered by the Government in forming the merger would be spread evenly around in the pre-existing seniority pecking order.

Although most airlines operated a bidline system, in BCAL it never evolved. Rostering was left to the operations department who allegedly spread the good and the bad evenly around. Inevitably there were rumours that certain pilots had been seen going into rostering with bottles of whisky, but, since nothing was ever proved, I put these rumours down to human paranoia. The stewardesses' work patterns were not so rigidly hidebound as the pilots and engineers, and if there was any toing and froing to be arranged it was usually manipulated in that department.

BCAL was a very gregarious and happy company, the morale was spectacular. Everybody in the company was cheerfully motivated into doing the best possible job with a smile on their face. We were much more than a clever Saatchi & Saatchi publicity blurb; we really were the world's favourite airline. We were the real thing.

A feature of this unsinkable morale was the crew party. On *every* nightstop someone would volunteer to host the crew party and we would clean up, bring our special crew price duty free booze, and muster for post flight R&R and the issue of our allowances. Allowances were paid by the captain to a laid-down scale, and this money was to be used for the purchase of meals in the hotel. But this was often confused in the wallet with the beer money and shopping cash. BCAL was a nightly on-going worldwide party.

I regret to say that these parties were often noisy, even raucous. Often other guests or the hotel manager would call and beg us to be more quiet, only to be inveigled by the girls to join the party. One night in the Karachi Intercontinental, Jim Southorn became unwell and had to be put to bed. Some unkind persons pushed his bed into the lift and Jim snored the night away in this elevating condition suffering only a sense of humour failure when he resurfaced in the morning.

Having admitted that a certain amount of alcohol was necked down route, it is relevant to reveal that the established alcoholic rule of thumb was no drinking within eight hours of call time, which rounded out to ten hours before take-off.

The law requires a pilot to be sufficiently rested before a flight, but the law does not explain how you can guarantee this commendable ruling when call time is 2200 (10 p.m.). The law requires you to go back to bed at 2 p.m. in the afternoon and somehow get eight hours of legal rest. In an environment of continual time zone changes and the necessity to attempt to adjust to these in order to get to sleep on demand, alcohol proved an indispensible aid.

So the crews were left to deal with the impossibility of it and handled the problem like adults. In thirty-six years of flying I never came across a drunken pilot or flight engineer on duty; a little subdued, maybe, but drunk, never.

Remember that these were the days before drink driving became measurable and enshrined in law. The query I am raising is which is the more dangerous? A desperately tired pilot? Or a rested pilot with a little bit of last night's party residual in the blood? I challenge the concept that this can make you incapable of a safe operation, and, thirty-five years later, I am here and retired, to prove it. I don't think my era could have survived without the assistance of social alcohol. The recent silliness where puritanical ground staff feel qualified to make operational safety judgements over the heads of top-quality men is absurd. These men have been arrested, fired and imprisoned while these ground staff are able to go home to their own little beds and have eight hours of top-quality rest between midnight and breakfast without first experiencing what a fourteen-hour duty day starting at midnight really feels like. Remember that we are considering the off-duty behaviour of top-quality men who took their role, their duty to do the safest possible job in a hostile environment, extremely professionally.

Today, such anti-social work schedules are handled by three pilots, with one free to have some horizontal rest in the crew bunk: the crew bunk for God's sake! Where were you when I needed you?

One of my favourite trips was LA. I liked the Californian 24-hour lifestyle and going out for either breakfast or dinner at 4 a.m., depending on what I felt like. We had a minimum 48-hour layover, but often we were off for days. There was a lot to see, such as the *Queen Mary*, Disneyland, Universal Studios, Mexico and many other delights. We used to go to the new huge convenience stores where you could get your meat, fish, bread, fruit, vegetables and groceries all in the same place. They were called supermarkets and we were all impressed with these and the general conclusion was that they might catch on.

Bringing home strawberries for Christmas might impress the neighbours, but it was impossible to solve the LA eight-hour time zone change at will. Scores of times I've laid tossing in bed, trying to sleep and dreading the arrival of call time, which would herald a fourteen-hour duty day beginning at your normal bedtime, knowing that I would be strapped in my seat in my blue pyjamas (my uniform) trying to stop my head falling off my shoulders for the next ten hours. Over the years I tried everything I could think of. In desperation I once tried a half bottle of red wine with a huge steak at lunchtime with only four hours to go before call time, but that didn't work either, but I could have ended up in jail.

If the most beautiful collection of hostesses were to be found in Southend-on-Sea, BCAL's girls in their different tartans came equal first.

We were proud of our company and I enjoyed marching through terminal buildings at the head of this band of steaming pulchritude watching blokes trip over their briefcases as our Caledonian girls floated passed. Besides the 'lookers' we had some quite spectacular characters. Two choice stories are both vehemently denied by the alleged parties involved. One was a special flight taking a party of celebrity golfers to a charity match at Gleneagles. The girls were drooling over Sean Connery and having attacks of the vapours. One comedian, famous for his diminutive stature, made a pass at one of our most spectacular girls.

'How do you fancy a little fuck?' he asked.

'No thank you,' she allegedly answered. 'I don't like little fuckers.'

On another flight, a 'suit' in Business Class was desperate to see what was going on beyond the First Class curtain. Unable to contain himself he pressed the call bell and asked the attending stewardess to tell him the difference between First and Business Class.

With a perfectly straight face she looked him in the eye and said, 'Apart from the blow job, nothing.'

Many of our trips involved long stopovers, so we would often cash in the hotel money, hire a couple of cars and go sightseeing.

One choice memory was a trip where we were supposed to position by airline from San Francisco to Vancouver and wait around for six days. I cashed the air tickets, hired three cars and we drove up the Pacific coast stopping in the Schoolhouse on the Creek in trendy Mendocino and a couple of beach resorts up the Oregon coast – a rolling party.

On another trip we went south from LA down the San Diego Freeway into Mexico. We were late and in a hurry, so the drill was that I would lead the way, and Ron Baxter in the following car was briefed to watch behind for prowl cars. The first indication that we had been clocked was when I saw the flashing red lights in front pulling me over. I stopped and Ron pulled in behind me. The patrolman got out of his car and came over. Without any prompting the girls were on the case. They jumped out of the two cars and surrounded the cop. 'Is that a real gun in your holster or are you just pleased to see me?' et cetera. The poor cop was surrounded by seven British dazzlers who didn't seem to be at all concerned about the gravity of 100mph plus on the freeway. The upshot was the week in jail was waived and a severe warning issued and humbly accepted.

We night-stopped in Ensenada, Mexico, on the coast of Baja California and the next day we headed inland to a place called Mike's Sky Ranch that we had heard about. After a couple of days riding horses, bouncing the dune buggy and playing cards we set out east to cross the Baja desert to come back via Mexicali. On reflection, after lunch was not a wise time to choose. The gravel road rapidly disappeared into just wheel tracks in the desert sand. It was late afternoon when we came to a double crossroads of tracks in the sand. One of these tracks out of the dozen was the right one, but which? I could see a range of mountains in the distant east and figured we needed to get through these at some stage to intercept the coast road to Mexicali. Then, in the hazy distance I noticed that there appeared to be a pass through, so I chose the track that pointed in that direction. It got dark, but we glued ourselves to the tyre tracks in the sand, beginning to worry that we were going to spend the night in the desert, cold, lost and running out of fuel. After a couple of hours we left the desert behind and noticed we were back on a gravel road going through some mountains. Then much to my relief we hit concrete going north-south. This had to be the Mexicali road so, thanking our lucky stars, we followed it in and took the first motel we came to.

In Singapore I used to enjoy taking the girls to Bujis (Boogie) Street. Bujis Street by day is just a junction like any other in the city, but by night the tables came out and the area becomes transformed into garish restaurant bars. Five-year-old boys would swarm around like flies challenging you to a game of noughts and crosses for a dollar. It was certain humiliation to accept.

The venue was a favourite for all the sex-starved sailors passing through this maritime crossroads of the East who had come ashore looking for assorted mischief, rest and relaxation. It was always likely that fights would break out and bottles thrown, so I used to brief the crew, in event of trouble, stand up, face outwards and look menacing with a beer bottle in your hand.

We would head for Fatty's pavement restaurant and gorge on dim sum, satay and assorted local delicacies. When replete, we would head around the corner and get a table as near to the public toilet as was still available. These toilets were a nondescript brick construction with a flat concrete roof. Its attraction as a preferred venue was to observe all kinds of unlikely sights to be seen going in. The whole point of Bujis Street was that it was the Mecca for all the ladyboys of the Far East. You might go for a leak and find yourself standing next to one of the most beautiful woman you had ever seen, or perhaps a stoker who would not look out of place in a rugby scrum if it wasn't for the lurid dress, stiletto heels and lipstick.

But the prize of the evening was to chance upon a sailor's fire dance.

God alone knows what sequence of events might trigger a sailor's fire dance, but suffice it to say that it began with the appearance of two sailors on the concrete roof of the toilet who would strip naked. This in itself would excite reactions of amazement amongst our girls but what followed would cause them to doubt the evidence of their own eyes.

The next step of the dance was that each sailor would get a sheet of *The Straits Times* and roll it into a cone shape like an old fashioned loud hailer. The narrow end was then twisted into a point and thrust up his anus. (This is true.) Then each would set fire to his opponent's newspaper and they would prance colourfully about on the concrete roof like sumo wrestlers until the situation became too hot for the loser.

I cannot begin to describe some of the expressions I have seen on the girls' faces as they experienced a sailor's fire dance. You had to be there, but I have cried real tears. As one girl said, 'I don't think my mother will believe this.'

Sadly Singapore's Prime Minister, Lee Kuan Yew, decided that this kind of exhibition was not the sort of thing he wanted his tourists to see and the whole thing was closed down. The ladyboys relocated to Bangkok taking many of the tourists with them.

Making the most of our trips was a regular feature among BCAL crews. From Lima, many went 12,000 feet up the Andes to see the ruined Inca city of Machu Picchu. From São Paulo, others went to see the spectacular waterfalls at

Iguazu. Scuba diving in Barbados was popular as was the wildlife in the various game parks around Nairobi.

I never quite got to the bottom of Nairobi. Was Nairobi naturally full of beautiful women or did it attract beautiful women? Or, conversely, did women become more beautiful in Nairobi; was there something in the air? Having a beer on the stoop of the *Norfolk Hotel* watching all that semi-wild life go by was time well spent. Whatever the answer was, the women there were mesmerizingly attractive, just like the exotic local flowers, bird life and safari parks. Just about every trip the hotel messenger boy would be seen trawling the lounges with his message board paging for a Doctor Livingstone.

Something about Kenya and Uganda seemed to bring about an eruption of the hormones. Every time we arrived in Entebbe or Nairobi the bottom of the aircraft steps would be besieged by 'the cowboys'. Cowboys were the local expatriates who were desperate for feminine company. This vacuum suited the girls perfectly and they allowed themselves to be taken out for dinner and treated like goddesses.

One famous cowboy was a friend of mine called Jean. Jean was a musician from Switzerland who began his career in the Folie-Bergère. After the Folie he got himself a piano bar job in Hong Kong. It was there he became fascinated with flying and he got himself a Commercial Pilot's Licence at the local flying club, which was run by off-duty Cathay Pacific pilots. After one or two dubious jobs flying 'stuff' around Africa, the licence got him to Nairobi flying the DC9 with East African Airways.

Jean stoutly maintained that he was just a simple Swiss boy being used by those sophisticated English airline hostesses. He married one of our feisty Irish girls called Maureen and they enjoyed a fiery relationship.

Slow to adjust to married life, Jean decided to go skiing with the boys in Switzerland, which caused a reaction from Maureen. When his car refused to start he discovered that all the plug leads had been severed with the pruning shears.

Furious, he set out to walk to the village to get the bus, lugging his suitcase in one hand and skis over his shoulder. Maureen was hysterical and told the housemaid that the master was leaving them. The housemaid became distraught and sprinted down the road. Sobbing, she wrapped herself around one of Jean's legs. 'Oh Master, don't leave us'. Jean was having trouble leaving anyway, with a heavy suitcase in one hand, skis over his shoulder and a housemaid clinging on his leg like a club foot.

Jean's other passion was shooting and he is a champion shot in Switzerland where shooting is more serious than football. So, between flying and hunting, Kenya suited him to perfection. One day, after a hunting trip and another 'domestic' dispute, Maureen locked him out of the house. Livid, he hammered on the door, but she wouldn't let him in. So, as you would, he shot the door down. By which time Maureen was hiding under the bed terrified that she was going to end up shot, stuffed and mounted on the wall in between the springbok and the impala.

When I first went to Africa it was still part of either the French or British Empires and a strong colonial administration was in place and working fairly well. With independence, this organization began to crumble, and some countries reverted to the kind of tribalism that spawned the genocide in Rwanda.

For the airlines the effect of this fragmentation was that there was no longer a unified air traffic control over Africa. The nation states provided reasonable air traffic services inside their borders, mainly because the airlines paid them for the use of their airspace by the minute, but there was no overall control and the border transits were potentially dangerous. In the end the airlines had to evolve their own backup service and all crews were recommended to broadcast their flight details on an unofficial dedicated frequency. This was far from satisfactory. I recall one night noticing that two aircraft, operated by UTA and Air Cameroon, were broadcasting an arrival time over Bamako at the same time and at the same height. When they didn't seem to notice this for themselves I called them up and suggested they communicate. I regret to say that, as far as I am aware, this unsatisfactory system still prevails and is an accident just looking for a place to happen.

As a result of the merger with BUA, BCAL now had South American routes. This was a very agreeable slip pattern. The first sector was to either Madrid or Lisbon for a couple of days. The next sector was to Rio de Janeiro for another couple of days followed by a three-sector day to São Paulo, Buenos Aires and Santiago in Chile and then the reverse back home. Outbound in Madrid I used to buy a box of Cuban cigars and a bottle of Carlos III, my favourite brandy. These would last me all around the slip in baronial style.

The company inherited some South American stewardesses and on my first trip back to Brazil, when one came into the cockpit, I told her I was very excited about going back to where I was born. 'Where exactly were you born?' she asked suspiciously. So I told her I was born in Niteroi, which was a ferry ride across the bay. Ah, she said sadly. You are not a Carioca, you are a Fluminense. Fluminense are the dumb ones from over the water. What a pity to get so close to perfection and just miss.

In my mother's papers I found a post card from me to my father from Rio de Janeiro. The gist of this was:

Dear Dad,

I know you always wanted me to be a sailor, cruising the South American coast with a weather eye open for a rich ranchero's daughter, and I know I broke your heart when I left the job you would have killed for. But here I am flying up and down the South American coast in a 707 with a weather eye open for a rich ranchero's daughter. Will this do?

Life was just about perfect for a South American baron and I could have stayed on the route for life. There were only two worries. One worry was that flying practically north–south, sooner or later you had to cross the intertropical front. The ITF is the weather system that separates the northern and southern climatic hemispheres. The ITF was usually defined by a solid line of thunderstorms that you had to find a way through. Sometimes you had to fly down the line for hundreds of miles before you found a likely looking gap.

Although the radar was extremely accurate at showing storm cells, my one fear was that we would chance upon a thunderstorm in the process of creation. Several times I have seen thunderstorms break out before my eyes. An innocent-looking cloud suddenly explodes like milk on the boil. Good though the weather radar is it would not be so good for something like a geyser boiling up from beneath.

The second worry was the Andes, graveyard of innumerable aircraft. At over 20,000 feet, the Andes are high enough to be mostly snow covered. In the early days, with a shortage of radio beacons for navigation, it was tempting to try and stay visual, and it was then that the snow-topped mountain were at their most dangerous, disguising themselves as clouds. But the most feared feature of an Andes transit was the ever-present possibility of severe turbulence caused by moderate Pacific winds being suddenly forced to rise 20,000 feet. I never experienced an extreme of turbulence but many colleagues did. The drill that evolved was that all the galley equipment would be stowed away or lashed down and the seat belt signs would go on. No sooner had you crossed the mountains than you had to descend to sea level to land at Santiago without the luxury of radar, so a very tense cockpit would meticulously check and cross-check position while descending to the transitory safety heights – with the Andes looming over your shoulder like an axeman.

Life as a Boeing 707 captain produced many choice moments. One I remember particularly was when we were performing a series of immigrant charters for the Australian government. We would pick up immigrants somewhere in Europe, such as Athens and Belgrade, and fly them to Sydney or Melbourne. Usually we went back empty, which was the perfect excuse for the chief steward to order in the best Sydney lobster for the crew meals.

Then some spoilsport in sales noticed all these empty sectors and had a bright idea. The upshot was that instead of going home with empty seats and lobster-replete bellies, I was rostered to bring a party of nouveau riche Australian/ Maltese home to Malta for a visit.

Something like twenty years previously, these Maltese immigrants had said goodbye to their friends and relations to start a new life in Australia, which in those days seemed like it was on another planet. They never expected to ever see each other again. But after twenty years in Australia, they had made a bit of spare cash.

So we duly landed in Luqa and taxied up to the gate. I could see a crowd of people on the roof of the old terminal. As I shut down the engines the sky suddenly erupted into a display of colour and noise filled with rockets, roman candles, Catherine wheels and thunder flashes. This crowd was waiting to see friends and relatives that they never expected to ever see again and they were celebrating like they had come back from the dead. I just sat there dazed, aware, perhaps for the first time, that besides flying around the world having a good time for myself, I was actually doing something useful; I was helping to bring families and friends together, something that was so joyous to them that their feelings were exploding like a new millennium firework extravaganza.

On another trip we were coming back from Bangkok. It was summer, so the jet streams were weak. If all went to flight plan I hoped we could squeeze it back to Gatwick without a refuelling stop. All did go well as far as top of climb when the chief stewardess came up and said that one of the passengers, a young girl, was having trouble breathing. I went back to have a look at her and she was definitely in trouble. She was lying in the doorway breathing oxygen. Each breath she took looked and sounded like her last. I was not anxious to dump forty tons of fuel and go back, so I said I would reduce height enough to keep the cabin pressure something like sea level, and see if that helped. After getting air traffic control clearance to descend, her mother reported that she was breathing easier so we pressed on, but the lower altitude was now eating into my precious fuel reserves.

We were coming up to the Mediterranean when the chief stewardess again came up and said she really didn't like the look of the girl, so I went and had another look. Sure enough, she looked just a few gasps short of terminal. I said to the mother that I thought the best thing to do would be to land at Athens and they could get home overland from there.

'Don't worry about her,' the mother said. 'She'll be okay. I've seen it all before.'

I thought this was a little unmotherly, but I went along and we pressed on to Gatwick.

As always, when you are short of fuel, the weather turns bad and Gatwick was fogbound. We set out to divert to Cardiff when the company called in and said they would prefer Stansted, which was reporting weather well above landing limits. We recleared back to Stansted and by now the fuel state was getting critical. We needed to get down at Stansted. I had spent my life arranging not getting into positions where there are few options left.

I glued myself onto the ILS; we were going to land off this one whatever the weather. As it happens the weather was good and we landed at Stansted without any further problems. I taxied to the stand and as the passengers got off and I asked the chiefie how our sick girl was.

'Huh!' she snorted. 'As soon as the door opened, she threw off the oxygen mask, jumped to her feet and was off down the stairs and across the tarmac like a groupie after the Beatles. There wasn't even a backward glance, never mind a thank you for all our trouble.'

It seems that mothers know best.

On another trip we were coming out of Vancouver for Gatwick and were treated to an unusually spectacular display of aurora borealis (Northern Lights). The sky in front of us was transformed into a shimmering white devil's mask, and we appeared to be aiming right into its mouth. It was eerie.

Another strange story is when I was positioning to Santiago to replace a captain who had gone sick. The only seat available was in Air France first class. I was sitting behind two Americans who were at the 'talking loudly' phase of French hospitality and they obviously felt it safe to talk freely in English on a French aircraft. They seemed highly delighted with the success of their tactics to undermine Allende's socialist government. If I understood correctly, their tactic was to offer more escudos to buy dollars. Every day they offered more and more escudos to buy dollars. This was designed to make the Chileans insecure with their own currency and to try and buy the dollars, which were rising in value daily.

This tactic seemed to be working well because the local traders were prepared to sell anything to get dollars; the crews were going home with unbelievable bargains. One night we hired the hotel limo from the *Cristobal Sheraton* and went to *Il Perron*, a classy steakhouse in Providencia, across the river. We had a great meal, wine and the limo back to the hotel. The cost was less than a dollar each. I repeat we each had change from one dollar. A few weeks later the socialist President Allende was killed in a rocket attack on his palace by the Chilean Air Force. The new regime promised to restore stability, and in his own inimitable way, Admiral Pinochet did just that.

On another long Hong Kong stopover the girls were all excited at the prospect of unlimited cheap shopping. At the crew party I briefed them about never paying the asking price in Hong Kong, but to bargain and haggle. Tell them you are airline crew, not rich tourists.

A Cathay Pacific friend loaned me his huge American car and we all crammed in for a tour of the colony. There was an ancient Chinese walled town beyond the mountains that formed the background for Kowloon. After that we went for a tour of the border area to see if we could see any Red Guards.

As we approached the border we came to a police post with a raised barrier. Since nobody was around we drove on through until we came to long, high chain-link fence rather like a tennis court. Peering through this we could see some Red Guards strutting about on the Chinese side. Then all of a sudden we were deluged by the army and police and found ourselves under arrest for illegal entry into the border zone. After a couple of hours we were released but ordered to appear before the Fanling Local Magistrates Court in the morning.

The next day we arrived as instructed and I explained to a local police inspector that if the barrier hadn't been raised and the post deserted we would never have trespassed.

'Don't worry,' he said. 'I advise you to plead guilty and you'll probably get off with a token $20 fine (£1.50).'

So I briefed the crew to plead guilty and we waited our turn while a Chinese chef was remanded in custody for butchering his wife. We stood in line in front of the Magistrate and all pleaded guilty. To my disgust, because it wasn't our fault, we were all fined $200 each.

One of our girls, Beryl Hulme, was aghast. It was a serious curtailment of her shopping options. 'What about the crew discount?' she demanded hotly. The court session was suspended for several minutes while we all recovered.

In the end I paid all the fines because the crew had all pleaded guilty on my instructions. I had a bit of trouble with the chief pilot when I claimed all the fines (except mine) on my expenses, but he accepted my reasoning that I had ordered the crew to waive their rights to a fair trial in two weeks' time in favour of having a crew to fly the aircraft home on schedule.

On another trip we were in Honolulu waiting for a horse freighter on the way home from Melbourne. We hired a car for a drive around the island and on the way we saw some Yanks jumping off a cliff hanging underneath a kite. These were the very first hang-gliders. Mike Winterkaines and I got very excited and resolved to try out this new sport. Back home, we drove to Marlborough and bought one of these contraptions from a pioneer enthusiast.

Initially we played safe and attempted to fly it from gentle safe slopes, but all we did was crash the kite and bend the aluminium tubes that it was made from. We realized the best way was from a really steep slope to give us the air room for the clumsy learning curve.

We chose the Devil's Dyke on the Downs behind Brighton. On the first launch just about everybody froze on the bar and performed a neat 180, crashing back on the hill not too far from where you took off from. On my second jump I managed to overcome my terror and move around the bar so as to steer the machine. The problem was that the seat was a slippery plastic swing seat such as you might find on a cheap child's back garden swing, and I slipped right off this seat. Luckily I was holding the bar outside of the two swing ropes or I would have fallen off. Instead, the seat rode up to my shoulder blades with the two swing ropes tight in my armpits. In this less than ideal position I manoeuvred down to the field 600 feet below and performed a controlled crash because my arms were not long enough to apply the required elevator control. For all future rides I used to strap the seat securely to my backside with an elastic luggage hook-strap.

In hindsight it was amazing that one of our group wasn't killed. My closest call was a launch off the dyke with the intention of landing in the field the other side of a copse of trees. To my horror I found a downdraft and realized that I wasn't going to get beyond the trees and was going to run out of glide angle in the middle. I figured that if air would hold a hang-glider aloft, the twigs of a tree should do the job just as well – so long as I didn't bounce off, so as I landed on top of a tree I grabbed at a branch and made sure I stayed there.

The rest of our suicide squad ran down the hill and we debated how I was going to get down from forty feet up a silver birch tree. We had some climbing rope and somehow I managed to lower myself down to the ground, leaving the other end of the rope tied to the nose of the glider so we could pull it out of the tree once I was safely grounded.

After sorting out all the bits and pieces we went to *The Shepherd and Dog* pub to celebrate a pint of life. At the bar a bloke came up to me and said, 'Have you heard the rumour? There's a story going round that some BCAL captain crashed his hang-glider and got stuck in the trees.' I looked him in the eye and admitted that I had heard the same rumour.

In the mid-1970s BCAL suffered a horrendous cutback caused by an equally horrendous directorial cock-up. To manage our new route to New York, the company had set up an administrative structure in America that was so expensive that a much smarter accountant calculated that even if the airline sold every available seat on the aircraft, the company would still fail to break even. Confronted with yet another survival situation the company was forced to stop operating this cream of all routes, which let in Freddie Laker's Skytrain.

My method of dealing with BCAL's financial fragility was to always have another job up my sleeve. This led to the most comprehensive series of interviews I ever experienced with the end result of possibly joining Japan Airlines.

The presentation of likely candidates was handled by IASCO of San Francisco whom I had seen on my way home from Hong Kong. This time I had command experience. The process was in three parts. Part one was a visit to SFO for a medical examination and perusal of licences and log books et cetera. Part two came several weeks later with a trip to Moses Lake in Washington State where Japan Airlines had positioned a DC8-30. The DC8-30 was the extra-long version – so long that the rotate (the lifting off of the nosewheel) had to be performed in two stages to avoid scraping the tail end on the runway. There was an initial rotate to ten degrees (it might have been fifteen) and a wait until the final minimum flying speed was achieved. The training captain whose name I did not register – to my everlasting regret – was a veteran of the Pearl Harbor attack of 1941. He was a very practical pilot with a very practical way of establishing whether you could fly or not. I took off with the two-stage rotate and climbed to 15,000 feet. At which point I was asked to make a sixty-degree banked turn. The whole of civil aviation organizes its procedures on thirty-degree banked turns; sixty degrees in an airliner is nosebleed country. It is tricky because of the huge elevator trim changes involved. There are pilots flying today that have never been beyond forty-five degrees, ever. Somewhere in the murky depths of fighter pilot memory I recalled the way to manage sixty-degree turns on instruments. I trimmed into the turn and maintained level altitude not with the usual elevator, but by increasing or decreasing the angle of bank slightly.

I was passed on to phase three, but there were some unfortunate candidates from a company that had gone bankrupt who got themselves into difficulties; blokes who desperately needed the job but who hadn't flown for a year. Phase three involved a final interview in Tokyo. This was the most thorough examination I was ever to go through. In one test I was taken to a soundproof room where I laid on a couch while electrodes were attached to my chest. I presumed this was to be a standard ECG heart test. I was left alone for what seemed like ages while the traces registered the state of my heart. It was difficult to stay awake it was so peaceful. Then suddenly all hell broke loose. Bells rang, lights flashed, horns blared and there on the ECG traces was a record of my heart's response to an emergency situation. How Japanese is that! Not only did they measure how high I jumped, but also how quickly I recovered.

For the next step I was presented with a huge sheet of paper about two feet square. The page was set out in lines and columns of simple arithmetic problems, $5+7=, 6+9=, 2+4=$ et cetera all across the page from left to right and top to bottom.

The problem set was to perform as many of these simple additions as possible in twenty seconds. The page was deliberately set too wide to complete a whole line within the time limit, and so on down the page with a break of ten seconds before starting a new line.

Anxious to do well, you finish line one. On line two you are getting the hang of it and you get much further towards the right margin. Line three is even better. On line four you reach your limit and line five is the same.

Then you start to think 'Look here, I'm a bloody airline captain, not an accounts bookkeeper' and the next line plunges. Angry with yourself, the next line is also a disaster. Then you start to think, 'I'm here because I may need this job.' And the next line picks up, and the next and the next until you are back up to maximum levels.

By joining up the ends of the lines, a curve is produced that shows how quickly and efficiently you pick up a task, how fast you develop, how quickly you get bored, and how long it takes you to get back on performance. The curve is a picture of your work performance and personality. How diabolical is that?

The final phase was the interview with the directors and chairman of Japan Airlines, Mr Tanaka himself, the Prime Minister's son.

I recount this precisely, just to demonstrate how stupid I can be. I was determined to be cool and relaxed and was surprised when it was the entire Board that seemed to be all tensed up, not me.

I was invited to sit down and we proceeded with the usual interview questions. They were most interested in my personal life. I explained that my marriage was long over, and no, I didn't have a girlfriend at the moment. I pointed out that Tokyo was a huge international city that I was familiar with from Cathay Pacific days, so I didn't think that would be a problem. I thought I was doing okay because the Board now seemed relaxed and agreeable.

Then the interview was over, and the whole Board tensed up again. They were practically falling off their chairs. I thanked them for their consideration and left the room.

I was no sooner outside than my stupidity fell on me like a wall. In Japan, you should bow to your superiors as you go in, and you should bow as you come out. So I don't know for sure why I failed my Japan Airlines interview. Perhaps it was for being a bit slow on the uptake of Japanese customs, or it was for not having a girlfriend.

If the problem was the latter, as a typical instance of the fickle finger of fate, I flew Japan Airlines back to London and the next day was rostered for a Far East slip where, at a party at the sheikh's summer palace in Bahrain, I met again the love of my life, Glenda, one of those exceptional beauties from Southend-on-Sea and my roving days were over. It was just too late to influence Japan Airlines.

At around this time the Inertial Navigation System (INS) arrived and navigators were replaced by a black box. Overnight some great professionals and very good friends became extinct, an awful thing to happen in the middle of a career.

The INS is a gyroscopic system. When a force (movement) is sensed by a gyro it precesses to an amount equivalent to the strength of that force. The computer then converts that precessional force into direction and speed and refines that into a continuous readout of latitude and longitude. The incredible thing is the accuracy from such an unlikely concept. After every trip a measure is taken of the difference between your actual latitude and longitude and where the INS said you were. It was very rare to find an error greater than ten miles. On a 5,000-mile London to Los Angeles sector, an error of ten miles is equivalent of an error of about a fifth of one per cent; this is roughly equivalent to regularly scoring a bull's eye with a dart thrown from about one hundred metres.

One of the pre-flight functions of the navigators was to prepare the flight plan. The flight plan lists the direction and distance between each sector of the proposed flight. Application of the forecast wind establishes the time for each sector from which it determines how much fuel will be required for the actual trip. To this is added forty-five minutes' holding time in case of bad weather or congestion plus enough for the proposed alternate airfield in case the destination airfield weather is below landing limits and, finally, a 5 per cent contingency reserve. The whole is then totalled and the final figure is offered to the captain who adds a couple of tons extra for Mum and the kids, and the resultant figure is sent to the refuellers to load the aircraft.

This function of the navigator was taken over by a computer based in California. The company operations department would request a flight plan for a particular aircraft type between any two places in the world, and minutes later a computer plan would arrive. By necessity, this computer would have to estimate the wind direction and strength at the upper levels of the atmosphere. These plans were also extremely accurate. I have never understood how a computer programme could so accurately estimate the wind strength and direction at 35,000 feet over the middle of the Atlantic Ocean, but it did to an incredible accuracy; not quite as good as the INS, but rarely badly wrong. The arrival of INS and the computer plan were the two principal factors that transformed aviation from man's work into a science, an automation; the black boxes were taking over.

However, the black boxes could let you down. I was rostered for a freighter to Lagos. It had been raining all night and we took off into sullen sky. At lift-off speed (called VR), as we rotated into a flying attitude, everything suddenly went quiet as we lost everything. There was no radio, either incoming or outgoing, so we automatically switched to the radio failure drill, which involved following the SID (Standard Instrument Departure) as cleared, switching the transponder to radio failure code, then following the flight plan as filed. This involved climbing up to 29,000 feet in the direction of France. The problem was that we had lost the VORs (a primary navigational aid) as well. Such a complete catalogue of failures was absolutely unique in my aviation experience.

Even though we still had the INS, I was not happy about continuing the flight as planned as the radio failure procedure called for because, with so many failures already, what other failures might be in store? Was the pressurization going to work? Without knowing what the problem was, it seemed unwise to attempt anything that involved reliance on the suspect aircraft systems for survival.

I decided that we would return to Gatwick and turned towards Mayfield, which was still available on one of the NDBs. Blindly, I radioed my intentions and asked for clearance to go to Mayfield and hold. There was no answer, but I heard a background noise that came and went, like a response, but with no voice. I called again and told air traffic control that I could hear a feedback crackling noise, but no voice. If that is you Gatwick, count to five seconds and respond. After five seconds the feedback came and went again. I told them that I thought they were receiving me, but I was not receiving them. Count five seconds and confirm. Again, after five seconds the feedback came and went so I described what had happened and that I intended to go to Mayfield at 4,000 feet to hold and dump fuel prior to returning to Gatwick. Was this approved? After five seconds the feedback came and went as before. So I dumped 40 tons of fuel in the Mayfield holding stack. As we dumped, the radio began to pick up intermittently and gradually improved until it seemed to be fully restored. We re-established two-way communications, completed the dump and landed back at Gatwick without further hindrance.

Back on the stand we were the object of considerable interest and every engineer on shift was available to solve the mystery.

It didn't take long. The aircraft had been loading the freight during heavy rain. With the huge cargo door open, inevitably some rain had got into the aeroplane, leaked down into the hull then accumulated in the nose, which is the lowest part of the aircraft on the ground. This water had collected into a considerable puddle in the nose, and when we rotated the nose on take-off the water was sprayed over all the electronics in the electronics bay and shorted everything. As the flight progressed, the water began to evaporate, allowing the radios to restore.

The co-pilot, Dave Shadbolt, was magnificent throughout. Anything I suggested he was either in the process of doing, or had just done. I gave him a glowing commendation in my report. Needless to say, our experience was published in all the safety magazines that are circulated to every airline in the world and opening the cargo door in rain became a cautionary item.

One of the unique features of the aviation business is honesty and transparency. Every incident has to be reported to the Flight Safety Board where it is analysed and then published in the monthly magazine so that the rest in the industry can learn from the incident the easy way. In this way aviation technique becomes the combined experience of every individual airline in the industry, whereas hospitals, doctors, lawyers, industrialists and politicians seem to rely on prevarication, lies and spin, which might explain why all these professions make much slower progress in overdue improvements.

The success of aviation devolves in the main from the applied expertise of three professional bodies, the pilots, the engineers and air traffic controllers.

The main interface between pilots and engineers is the Technical Log, or Techlog as it is usually called. The Techlog is a legal document that contains a complete record of the aircraft's operational history. One is carried on the aircraft and a copy is held at base. In the event of an accident or incident the first item to be impounded is the Techlog. The Techlog records every minute of engine movement and is used to measure the accumulated hours of the engines and other time-lifed components before they must be removed for major overhaul. The Techlog is signed by the engineers who refuel the aircraft and those who repair any incoming defects, and finally by the captain when he has satisfied himself that everything that should be done has been done. After any flight, when the engines are shut down the captain will enter any aircraft defects that he has noticed during the inbound trip.

Another document vital in the pre-departure routine is the load sheet. If you imagine an aluminium bar suspended from the ceiling by a piece of string tied precisely in the middle, then you would expect the bar to hang horizontally. If you were to suspend various non uniform weights in various positions along this bar, by carefully adjusting the positions of these weights, you could ensure that the bar remains horizontal. The load sheet performs the same function for the aircraft and ensures the aircraft is loaded within certain established centre of gravity limits, which in turn ensures that the aircraft remains controllable for take-off, landing and the entire flight as perhaps sixty tons of fuel is burned off. With three hundred passengers in a six hundred-seat aircraft it would obviously not be a good idea if they all crammed into the rear three hundred seats.

The load sheet also totals the weight of the passengers, fuel and freight to make sure that the aircraft is not exceeding its maximum safe weight.

There are various weight limitations to be considered. Every aircraft has an absolute maximum allowable take-off weight known as its structural limit. If, for example, you overloaded an aircraft by twice its maximum, on take-off, the wings might take off, but leave the overloaded fuselage behind on the runway.

The most interesting, and most complex part of ensuring a safe take-off is arriving at the RTOW (Regulated Take-off Weight), which takes into account every possible factor affecting a take-off except stupidity. There are two main considerations, one, the airfield and runway itself, and two, the weather conditions being experienced on the day.

In considering the airfield, the principal consideration is the length of the runway. Obviously, the aircraft needs to get safely airborne before it runs out of concrete. Wind has the effect of increasing the effective runway length, and since wind can be gusty and variable, the RTOW calculations only allow half the wind speed to be taken into account. A gradient on the runway is also factored. If there is an uphill gradient it effectively reduces the available runway length, and a downhill gradient increases it. The other consideration of weather is the affect on engine performance. High pressures and low temperatures increase an engine's power output, and vice versa. All these factors are taken into account, either graphically, or by computer to arrive at a maximum safe RTOW.

But what if the aircraft has an engine failure before it reaches a safe flying speed? To be safe, the aircraft needs to have enough runway available to be able to accelerate to the minimum safe take-off speed, but also to have enough runway left to stop in if an engine should fail before reaching that minimum safe speed. This consideration is calculated from tables in the Performance Manual, which, taking into account all the previously mentioned factors, arrives at the three critical take-off speeds, V1, V2 and VR (V = velocity or speed).

V1 is the decision speed. If an engine fails before V1 the pilot must abandon the take-off, close the thrust levers and stand on the brakes. If an engine fails after V1 the pilot must continue the take-off.

VR is the speed at which the pilot pulls back on the control column to rotate the aircraft around the wheel axles so that it takes up a willing-to-fly attitude. What is happening is that the wings are now presented to airflow at an angle that produces lift from the wings – lift of a sufficient force to be able to carry the weight of the aircraft into the air.

V2 is the minimum safe flying speed when the aircraft, now rotated into a flying attitude, will begin to leave the ground. The aircraft continues to accelerate beyond V2 so as to increase the lift from the wings and increases all the safety margins.

If the runway faces an uphill slope in the after take-off climb-out area, this also has been taken into account. If the pilot loses an engine after reaching safe take-off speed, his weight will have been considered in the RTOW calculations to ensure that he can still climb to a safe height above any obstacles that might lurk in the initial climb-out flight path.

On take-off the non-flying pilot will call the three speeds in sequence, V1, VR and V2. Since this is the most critical part of the flight, the correct response to engine failures before and after V1 is practised exhaustively in the simulator. Pilots even practise the simulated death or incapacitation of the flying pilot, and the non-flying pilot is trained to quickly perceive the situation and continue with the appropriate drills, whether to stop or go depending upon whether V1 has been reached or not.

From the above paragraphs, the reader will have gained some comprehension of how much actual scientific measurement has superseded what used to be decisions made at the captain's discretion in the earlier years of my career.

The arrival of the flight simulator allowed a huge improvement in flight safety. The simulator is an exact reproduction of the cockpit of an aircraft type mounted on hydraulic jacks. These jacks can simulate aircraft movement in an extraordinarily lifelike way. Their advantage, besides being much cheaper to run than aeroplanes, is the facility to practise exercises that would be dangerous in a real aircraft. Similarly, at the flick of a switch, the instructor can relocate the aircraft to any of the major airfields in the world, not only the runway and landing aids, but also the view out of the window. I have flown a Boeing 747 in between Manhattan's skyscrapers in a simulator. So great has been the improvement in simulator performance that today, in many airlines, a pilot's first trip on the line with passengers is often his first trip in the real aeroplane.

So lifelike are these simulators that a pilot has to perform as if he were actually in an aeroplane in order to demonstrate the required level of proficiency. For example, in BCAL, for a time we used to use MEA's B707 simulator in Beirut. This early simulator misbehaved. The rudder bar was oversensitive and caused the world to jerk sideways left and right like a Richter force twenty earthquake. 'Just ignore that' our instructor called because it didn't affect the ILS.

For some exercises, such as a change of airfield, the aircraft has to be on the ground with the parking brakes on, so my instructor told me to just ignore the oscillating runway and land the aircraft from this approach. It is odd, but I just couldn't do it. Even though I knew it was only a computer image, I just could not put the aircraft down without a runway to land on – I just couldn't do it. To get the performance level required to pass the test you had to behave like it was for real.

A typical day
For transatlantic flights, because of the time zone changes and the need for the return sector to be an overnight flight, the take-off times out of London are usually at midday or later. A 2 p.m. Los Angeles flight will arrive at LAX at midnight, which is 4 p.m. local time. After a three-hour turn around the aircraft will leave at 7 p.m. local time, arriving ten hours later at 5 a.m. California time, which would be 1 p.m. London time. Transatlantic schedules are entirely governed by the need to arrive at the various destinations and back at sensible times.

For a Los Angles trip the crew will check in for duty an hour before take off at 1 p.m. In British Caledonian, the captain would first go to the cashiers and sign for the amount of dollars in cash and traveller's cheques that he had requested over the phone. The captain then goes to the flight operations room and meets the co-pilot and the flight engineer. Together they look at the weather forecast and computer flight plan. The computer will have already worked out the most economical route to fly. Because the Atlantic is so busy at this time, with all the European and returning American traffic, the Ocean Control Centre would have also looked at the upper winds and the best routes and registered four or five optimum tracks, one of which the airline will have to request to fly – obviously the most economical one. The NAT tracks (North Atlantic Tracks) options, usually identified as Alpha, Bravo, Charlie and Delta would parallel the most economical flight path with one degree of latitude (sixty miles) separation. The captain generally accepts the computer's assessment of the best flight plan and this plan is then filed with all the agencies, European, Oceanic, Canadian, Icelandic and American. The captain then decides on a final fuel load and may add a few tons of extra fuel should he consider, from his experience, that it might be needed due to factors that the computer does not consider, such as possible track diversions mandated by thunderstorm activity or extended holding delays caused by fog or high traffic density. This final fuel load is radioed to the refuellers on the tarmac. The operations officer also hands over the flight briefing folder, which contains all remaining factors relevant to the safe conduct of the flight, such as active danger areas. All military and commercial activity that might cause a hazard to any aircraft must confine its activity to registered danger areas and notify the Civil Aviation Authority, which relays such activity to all airport briefing rooms. The captain's flight brief also contains details of anything not covered elsewhere such as hazardous cargo requiring special consideration, live freight, or commercial factors, VIPs et cetera.

These pre-flight procedures take about twenty minutes and the flight crew then rendezvous with the cabin staff to be bussed out to the aircraft where the crew prepares the aircraft for departure. The chief stewardess is responsible for ensuring that the cabin is clean and prepared, that the catering is adequate for the expected numbers, that the in-flight entertainment is ready to go and he, or she, will check that all the safety equipment is on board and correctly stowed.

The flight deck crew then prepares the aircraft for flight. The inertial navigation system is started and loaded with all the waypoints (geographical positions) that the aircraft is required to fly over. The engineer gives the aircraft a thorough inside and outside check, and the co-pilot checks that all the required manuals, maps et cetera are on board.

All the aircraft systems are checked throughout the cockpit, every single one. As take-off time approaches the engineers will confirm that the aircraft has been correctly refuelled and that all defects the aircraft arrived with on the previous flight have been repaired or adjusted. They then sign the Technical Log, which is countersigned by the captain. The top copy is taken away by the ground engineer and filed. Meanwhile, the passengers have been embarked and the final load and balance sheets are brought for the captain's signature. The load sheet confirms the total number of 'souls on board', and that the aircraft is loaded to within its centre of gravity and maximum allowable take-off weight limits.

Using these final and accurate weights, the flight crew establish the crucial take-off speeds, V1, VR and V2 as described previously, using the aircraft type's performance manual. These figures are checked and agreed between the captain, co-pilot and engineer. The co-pilot will then call the air traffic control centre and advise them that the flight is ready for departure. This radio call initiates the flight's sequencing into the prevailing air traffic environment existing at the time and an estimated take-off time is issued. The airport's ground control will then issue a start clearance time so that aircraft arrive at the holding point for take-off in the correct sequence together with a departure clearance. For every runway on each high-density airfield, a particular departure route is laid down. These routes, known as SIDs (Standard Instrument Departure routes) are the precise flight paths for the aircraft to follow to take into account local terrain, noise abatement routes and other airfields in the vicinity and the subsequent sequencing into the prevailing traffic congestion on the day. The aircraft will request 'push back' clearance, which will be allowed as the ground traffic situation permits. When cleared the tug will push the aircraft away from the gate and the crew will start all the engines. When pushed back into the taxiway the tug driver will ask for the brakes to be applied and then he will disconnect the tow bar and drive clear. The co-pilot requests taxi clearance and the control tower will issue instructions as to the precise taxiways to follow to the take-off holding point at the end of the runway. As the aircraft taxis out the co-pilot will read out the pre-take-off vital actions, which checks and confirms that the aircraft is fully set up and ready to go. The chief stewardess will come to the cockpit and confirm the total number of passengers on board and that the cabin is ready for take-off.

The airport ground controller will advise the local area air traffic controller that the flight is ready and the area controller will judge when the aircraft is safe to enter into the air traffic congestion pattern of the day.

After take-off the flight becomes the responsibility of the radar controllers who monitor its progress through the declared flight plan and the crew climb the aircraft to the first cleared height. The aircraft is 'cleaned up' – wheels, flaps and leading edge slats are retracted allowing the aircraft to accelerate to the maximum speed for the cleared altitude. Usually, after take-off, the aircraft will be cleared to climb all the way up to its initial en route altitude. Hours later, as the aircraft burns fuel and gets lighter, the crews will request higher altitudes from air traffic control.

Once settled at cruise altitude and safely sequenced into the airways system the co-pilot will switch radio frequencies to Oceanic Control and request the flight's oceanic clearance.

Oceanic Control will then issue clearance on one of the listed tracks, and the co-pilot will read back the entire oceanic portion of the route with the captain monitoring to ensure there are no mistakes.

By this time the aircraft will be nearing its Oceanic Control entry point, usually the last bit of land such as Land's End, Shannon, Belfast, Glasgow or Benbecula, and the crew will switch to HF (long range) radio frequencies for all further position reporting points. One of the VHF (short range) radios will be switched to 121.5, which is the international frequency for distress messages to be ready for any incoming, or outgoing, distress messages, which will be picked up and relayed by other aircraft to initiate any search and rescue facilities.

There then begins a less hectic period of flight where a meal might be taken.

The aircraft has to make a position report upon crossing every 10 degrees of longitude, 20 west, 30, 40 and 50 west with the actual latitude. For example, the flight will report 'crossing 50 north and 40 west at flight level 330 (33,000 feet) at time 1407 zulu (GMT)'. At the same time the engineer will compare the actual fuel remaining and compare this with the computed flight plan figures to ensure the overall fuel integrity of the flight. The Oceanic Control will use the position information to monitor that a safe separation between flights is being maintained. The autopilot will be flying the aircraft and maintaining the height and track selected by the crew. The track will actually be defined by the INS. Before each reporting point the crew will check that the next sector track and distance are the same as that listed on the computer flight plan to ensure no degradation of the previously entered data. With three INS on board, navigational errors have become exceedingly rare.

Because of the shape of the world and that great circle tracks define the shortest possible distance between points, the North American entry points are usually in Canada; southern Canada, Gander, Halifax for east coast destinations and central Canada, such as Winnipeg and Moose Jaw for west coast cities.

For most of the years when I was flying the Cold War was a reality and extreme north Canada was the No Man's Land that faced Russia, so the entry and transit of the far north was particularly sensitive and the clearance to enter and the subsequent track keeping to cross had to be exact or you might find a couple of fighters on each wing tip.

On the flight, by the time lunch was over and the movie finished we were usually crossing the forty-ninth parallel and entering the USA and it would be time to talk to the passengers. This is a particularly featureless part of the world, but luckily, very often, we were passing over Billings Montana which has the distinction of hosting the Battle of The Little Bighorn where Colonel Custer met his famous Waterloo. I seized upon this feature so many times in my career and milked it that, as soon as I retired, I hired a car in Seattle and drove to Billings to evaluate the ground for myself.

As a point of interest, Custer's mistake was to disperse his soldiers into small pockets. This may have been good policy if expecting incoming artillery, such as he may have experienced in the recently ended civil war with the Confederates, but it was ill-advised against overwhelming Indian cavalry and these pockets of three or four men were simply overrun and massacred. The other half of the 7th Cavalry constructed a defensive position on the opposite end of the bluff and survived.

As the aircraft approaches destination the crews will become more animated, awakening from the torpor of long-haul. The pilots will have to work out where to begin the descent. A simple rule of thumb is that the aircraft needs a distance of three times the cruise altitude to descend at 3,000 feet per minute at speed plus ten miles to slow down to flap and slat extension speed, so an aircraft at 33,000 feet needs 99 miles to descend plus 10 miles to slow down, so the crew will ask for descent at 109 miles as measured on the DME (distance measuring equipment) from the destination airfield.

Before the descent begins the captain or flying pilot will brief the crew on the mountain safety heights around the destination airfield, the method he proposes to use for the approach, usually the ILS (instrument landing system), the height they should cross the outer marker (an NDB usually placed at about ten miles from the field on the extended centreline of the runway being used), the company listed landing minima for the particular landing aid and runway being used, and the lowest height he will be going to before abandoning the approach and overshooting if the runway is not in sight and a landing clearance given by the airfield tower. This briefing will also consider the state of the runway, i.e. whether it is wet and slippery and any other noted runway peculiarities such as up or downhill slopes and anything else relevant. In the event of an overshoot and missed approach, some airfields require an emergency turn to avoid obstacles. In other words, a very comprehensive consideration and revision takes place to ensure that all factors affecting the safety of a landing are taken into account.

In the event of bad weather or congestion, air traffic control might direct the flight into the holding stack at a particular height. The stack is generally a two-minute racetrack pattern around and towards an NDB with many aircraft stacked with a 1,000 feet vertical separation. The lowest aircraft in the stack will be cleared to make an approach, and when it is well clear all the other aircraft will descend 1,000 feet in sequence until it is their turn to make their approach.

As the aircraft slows down the crew will extend the slats and flaps, both are devices that change the shape of the wing, which allows it to fly more slowly, more safely. On the final approach the wheels will be lowered and checked that they are locked down in position by the illumination of three green lights on a dial on the instrument panel. In thirty-five years of flying I never had an undercarriage malfunction.

On touchdown the speed brakes will be extended, which dumps much of the lift of the wings so that the weight of the aircraft is passed to the wheels, which increases the efficiency of the brakes. Reverse thrust is selected on the engines, which also assists in the deceleration.

On the ground the aircraft will contact ground control who will direct them to their passenger unloading stand via particular taxiways so that inbound and outbound aircraft do not get in each other's way.

After the passengers, the crew then disembark and clear immigration and customs, just like everybody else, but with the advantage of using the quicker crew-only aisle.

Outside, the crew transport will be waiting to take the crew to the crew hotel. After check-in the crew will go to their rooms and it was usual in British Caledonian that the crews would remuster, together with their duty-free preference, in somebody's room where the captain would issue their allowances (money, usually dollars), for the purchase of three meals per day for the duration of the layover and some debriefing, rest and recuperation would take place. For the longer stopovers, arrangements might be made for sightseeing for those interested.

The purpose of this lengthy description of a flight is to give the reader an understanding of how thorough the flight safety and cockpit procedures are in today's flying environment, something all aviation employees regard with some pride and contributory satisfaction.

Twice in my life I have needed BALPA to come to my aid and both times they fell well below Perry Mason class. After the near miss over the seniority list after the merger with

BUA, I found myself rejoining BALPA (The British Airline Pilots Association) because I could see things that needed doing. My fellow pilots voted me to the PLC (Pilots Local Council), a position that was renewed every two years for the next sixteen.

My first target was the company pension scheme. I produced a paper that showed graphically that the assurance scheme administered by the Prudential was too much in the Pru's favour. It proved that a 'without profits' policy was merely giving you 45 per cent of the capital that our own contributions earned over twenty years, and even the 'with profits' policy only returned 55 per cent. I arranged a meeting with an independent insurance agent who advised the company to run its own pension fund, which was relayed to the directors and this was duly done. Caledonian's pension scheme evolved into one of the best in the industry.

I have already mentioned my theory that travel expands and sharpens the mind into innovation, and BALPA offered a great many opportunities to prove it by providing an endless supply of problems. One of my ideas was spawned by a deadheading flight home after twenty hours of positioning after a twelve-hour duty. I was so exhausted that I was practically unconscious in my club seat and when I was woken up for the landing my neck was stuck in a forty-five degree angle. If only you could stretch out in an aeroplane; if only aeroplanes were fitted out like Pullman sleepers.

The rationale behind the paper I proposed was that at Mach .82, today's jet liner, flying at the latitudes of the world's principal cities, tended to fly just a little behind the local time of the sun. So a jet leaving London at 10 p.m. local would arrive at New York at about 1 a.m. local time, and Los Angeles at about 4 a.m. local time, where it would day stop to leave at 10 p.m. to fly to Tokyo, Singapore, Dubai and London.

Such a schedule, flying exclusively at night, could employ one dedicated aircraft to be furnished with sleepers just like Pullman coaches. I suggested that such a service, perhaps called 'The Five Mile High Club', would monopolise first class travel.

Obviously, the idea was beyond BCAL alone, and my proposal was an operation in conjunction with an American carrier and Cathay Pacific Airways. Adam Thomson commended the idea, but regretted that he thought it was a bit beyond BCAL's scope, but the idea of proper horizontal rest was picked up by BA and the club and first class cabins were redesigned with couchettes. It was very popular, but the expensive use of space had to be reflected in the fares.

During the latter part of the 1970s under Jim Callaghan's premiership, paradoxically the unions were becoming suicidally belligerent. There were wildcat strikes that undermined the Labour Party's Government. This belligerency gradually escalated into the famous 'winter of discontent' with numerous self-defeating strikes. I was particularly nervous that these strikes would infect BCAL because the company's ever-fragile finances would not survive this kind of lemming-like disruption.

Having twice experienced company bankruptcies, and the trauma of household finances that these failures caused, and mindful of BCAL's perennial financial fragility, I wrote a paper for the PLC and the company proposing that we should have a 'contingency plan' whereby the workforce would be prepared to agree to accept an emergency pay drop to, say, half pay. My opinion was that a temporary period of half pay was preferable to bankruptcy involving an extended period on no pay; that any ensuing hardships could be quite simply relieved by the adroit use of those new fangled credit cards; and that the balance of salary unpaid could be repaid in some way, either by deferred pay, share issues, or pension additions.

Needless to say, the idea was unpopular amongst those who preferred the ostrich-in-head-sand, let's wait until it is too late, approach to liquidity problems.

The failure of the contingency plan idea led to one of my best ideas, which I presented in a paper to Adam Thomson, where I postulated that the current belligerence in the unions was not a negative trend, but a developing trend in union management relations. If the company launched a profit-sharing scheme, this would focus the workforce on earning profit as opposed to seeking unaffordable pay rises by confrontation.

Adam liked the idea but amended it. BCAL's perennial problem was that it was underfunded. Its principal backers were not really strong enough to fund the huge investments necessary for a successful international airline in aviation's volatile market place. As a consequence, after a good year, instead of expanding into opportunity, the company was always refunding last year's disaster. Adam could not afford a profit-sharing scheme so he brilliantly transposed it into a share profiting scheme. When the company made a profit, shares would be issued pro rata with salary and these shares could be converted on retirement. I was a little disappointed with this solution, which was not quite what I was suggesting, but when BA took over BCAL and we were each paid £12.50 a share and I cleared my mortgage, I was much more impressed with Sir Adam Thomson's instinctive business acumen.

BCAL was very union orientated and there was a liaison committee chaired by Alistair Pugh, the general manager, where unions were invited to air their grievances before they became problems. I frequently proposed that BCAL should consider a merger with Cathay Pacific to strengthen its financial position. Alistair said the idea was one that the company had under review. At one of these liaison meetings I mentioned that it was about time we aircrew knew who would be replacing Captain McKenzie (Mac) as flight operations director as he was approaching retirement.

The upshot was that I was called into the office to see Mac. To my amazement he asked me how I felt about being considered as flight operations director. I was completely taken aback because I had simply not considered such a move. There are pilots who spend their off days stalking the office, and others who are training captains with some idea of what went on behind the scenes. Frankly I expected Dave Page to get the job because he had been effectively running the airline for years. I did not consider that the fact he was a navigator, not a pilot, was of any relevance whatsoever. I was just a pushy ideas man who was a much better writer than he was a talker, so I said I thought the idea was 'too far, too fast'.

Immediately, Mac looked relieved with my response and the meeting was quickly concluded. I suspect the invitation had come from Adam himself and I suspect Mac had his own ideas about who he would prefer to see in the post.

While a bit of arm twisting wouldn't have gone amiss, I think my unpreparedness on receiving the offer is indicative of my unsuitability and political naivety. I thought, perhaps wrongly, that there were others better qualified.

How fickle is the finger of fate. A few weeks earlier, my late brother-in-law, Dr Charles Rondle, of the London School of Tropical Medicine, the man acclaimed for eradicating smallpox, published a paper by himself and 'an Airline Pilot', which earned him a front page spread in *The Sunday Times* colour magazine. The article lauded him as an extraordinary aviation detective.

I have already mentioned, from operating the Hadj, that our Arab passengers were somewhat baffled by our Western toilet arrangements and footprints revealed that they preferred the traditional squat standing on the toilet seat rather than sitting. Everybody knows about the use, or non use of the left hand in Eastern culture, and afterwards they would wash their hands in the washbowl.

In aircraft, toilet soil goes into tanks, which are emptied on each landing turnaround. Wash basin waste goes out into the atmosphere via drain masts on the underside. These drain masts are heated otherwise they would ice up as soon as the waste water encountered the minus 56°C temperature at 30,000 feet.

It occurred to me one day that the three mysterious outbreaks of cholera in Naples, Bahrain and Sarajevo were each downwind of a busy airway. I wondered if it could be possible that the cholera bacteria were originating from an infected passenger washing his hands and passing the bacteria out to atmosphere via the waste water drain masts.

I mentioned this to my brother-in-law at a dinner and Charles became very excited and said he would do some tests. The results showed that cholera bacteria would survive flash freezing at altitude and would be restored to virility in the warmer lower altitudes. And if they happened to fall into some area of the food chain, then an outbreak would be triggered.

Charles published his paper, not mentioning my name, he reasoned, in case the increased costs of extra water disinfection would prove embarrassing to my position in the industry. The paper was picked up by the media and Charles enjoyed a second five minutes of fame and the water carried in aircraft duly became more heavily sterilized.

The pity is that if he hadn't been so concerned for my position, it might have tipped the balance in my favour in the matter of the offer of Flight Operations Director and made Mac a bit more persuasively insistent. But I doubt it. It is not the missed opportunity of title, power and pelf I regret, but the fact that the incumbent directors did not show enough imagination to save the company from the resultant BA takeover.

I would have vigorously pursued a merger with Cathay Pacific, pointing out to Adrian Swire that he could not possibly know how the communist Chinese would react to capitalist companies when they reclaimed the colony. A merger with a London-based company would give Cathay a UK bolt-hole to withdraw to with the aircraft should the imminent return of Hong Kong prove to be a Chinese take-away. The same merger would give BCAL the backing of the Hong Kong and Shanghai Banking Corporation (HSBC) for the adequate financial backing that they never achieved. I would have vociferously argued that such a merger was mutually beneficial and would have banged heads together until it was achieved.

It is a great pity that the merger idea was not pursued more vigorously because HSBC backing would have saved us from being swallowed up by BA, which did little for the industry except leave a vacuum to be immediately exploited by Virgin Atlantic. I would not decry the enormous benefits in financial stability that accrued from the BA takeover; it is just a great pity that the magical *esprit de corps* of British Caledonian was not enshrined in the process. This was Lord King's biggest mistake.

After my unhappy experience with the BAC 1-11 training captains I could not get out of short-haul flights quick enough and bid for the DC10 as soon as I was able.

This led to missing an opportunity to get an interesting sideline in show business. While on short haul, with more regular hours, I took a television production and script-writer's course at Sussex University and had submitted a couple of sketches to the BBC's John Lloyd, producer of *Not The Nine O'clock News*. John replied that the present series was finished, but he would advise me when the second series was looking for material. His letter duly arrived, and I asked Kim Fuller, who was also on the same course, if he would like to join me in writing some scripts to John Lloyd's outline. Since Kim was a supply teacher earning very little and I was paying top rates of tax, we agreed that if we earned any money, he would take the first £15,000 and we would split anything on top, fifty-fifty. So as not to con-fuse the incoming cheques issue all the submissions were signed as Kim Fuller. We were just beginning to get some-where when the offer came to do the DC10 course in Dallas. I was so disillusioned with the Gestapo-like short-haul fleet training captains, I accepted. When I came back from Dallas a month later, Kim Fuller was up and running and, without a backwards glance, was writing sketches for Lenny Henry, Rowan Atkinson and Tracey Ullman et al.; excellent stuff. Kim's entrée into show business was tracked by his brother, Simon, who, memorably, rose to millionairedom managing the Spice Girls.

The DC10 course in Dallas was run by American Airlines (AA) who had all the latest training techniques. Each trainee had his own cubicle, which was fitted out with a tape deck and TV monitor through which the pupil could navigate the complexities of heavy jet systems and engineering at his own speed, so different from Cathay Pacific's desperately dull technique.

The trickiest part of the DC10 course was the adjustment to a greater degree of automation than before. It was a time when the pilot was handing over control of the aeroplane to the avionic systems. Instead of the pilot flying the plane, the plane was flying itself and the pilot was merely feeding instructions into the autopilot. Although this sounds easier, in fact it isn't because it was contrary to the nature of the hands-on pilot and there were hundreds of pretty coloured lights, knobs and switches to get mixed up.

Inevitably, in time it all began to fall into place and the new ways became more comfortable. Of interest, on my final checkout on the real aircraft we were waiting for take-off at Stockton, California, when I noticed that number 2 engine oil pressure was reading zero. I pointed this out to the check captain and a huge discussion developed about what this really meant. So much nothing was done that in exasperation I shut the engine down since bearings starved of oil have a tendency to seize up expensively. What may be of interest to the reader is that in ten years on the DC10 that was the only time I shut down an engine with a potential failure. I once shut down an engine as a precautionary measure after a lightning strike, but in ten years of constant flying I never had a genuine engine failure in the DC10.

The only genuine engine failure that I heard about in the DC10 resulted in a most spectacular demonstration of airmanship. At 37,000 feet a United Airlines DC10-10 suffered a catastrophic failure of number 2 engine (the one in the tail) on a flight between Denver and Philadelphia. As a result they lost all the hydraulic fluid, which meant that Captain Al Haynes and co-pilot Bill Records had no normal control of the aircraft; the control column was just a useless lump of metal. Just to make life more difficult, there was a residual rudder input that was inching the aircraft to the right. Luckily, on board was a deadheading training Captain Dennis Fitch who offered to help, which gave them an extra pair of hands. They were able to counteract the right turn with asymmetric power. To descend they had to reduce power on the remaining two good engines, and to turn left or right they had to apply asymmetric power. They were assisted in this by the incredible natural stability of the DC10. Somehow they managed to manoeuvre themselves into a long final approach into Sioux City Gateway Airport in Iowa. It is very difficult to land in the clean configuration, i.e. with no flaps and slats extended on the wing to help you slow down. The aircraft just floats and floats down the runway. (I know this because I tried it in the simulator.) Unfortunately, things started to go wrong in the final few hundred feet and the residual turn in the rudder caused a last-minute bank, which they couldn't control, and the aircraft cartwheeled down the runway and burst into flames. Some 111 passengers were killed, but 185 survived. When the engine exploded, there were 296 people at 37,000 feet in a flying coffin. That 185 survived is quite the most incredible feat of cool, brilliant airmanship I have ever heard about.

The Boeing 707 had almost as good engine reliability. I shut one down over the Atlantic because it was losing oil, and had one genuine failure over Prestwick en route to New York. There were two or three quite violent explosions that shook the aircraft. We identified number 4 engine, shut it down, dumped the fuel and returned to Gatwick.

Another interesting experience was a trip to Saudi Arabia. My co-pilot was Barbara Harmer. I flew the first leg, so Barbara was on the radio. In Saudi Arabia women are not allowed to drive cars, so I was fascinated to discover what the Saudis would make of a female DC10 pilot because if she had been a Saudi, the mob might have carried her off and stoned her to death for the impertinence. We duly arrived at the capital Riyadh and taxied up to the stand. I think the whole airport staff arrived and a huge crowd was waiting at the bottom of the steps; hundreds of Saudi men were waiting to see this Islamic anachronism. I was delighted to have put one more nail in the coffin of male chauvinism, but there is still a long way to go before Arab women are accorded their long overdue dignity of equality.

During the Falklands War I was rostered for a Lima slip, which involved a San Juan layover for a couple of days followed by a three-sector day to Caracas, Bogota and Lima with a seven-day layover. The fleet was heading south and there were anti-British demonstrations in Lima.

The chief pilot, Goff Bowles, met me in the operations room to discuss my reservations. I said that, in view of the riots, I would prefer to operate the route as planned, but the crew would withdraw with the aircraft and come back to San Juan as a passenger for the rest days. Although this would involve a technical violation of the maximum duty day, I didn't think the CAA would prosecute in view of the wartime circumstances, particularly as sitting in first class reading the newspapers was only technically duty time and hardly fatiguing. Goff convinced me that the company had the situation under constant review and that we should play it off the cuff as we saw it on the day.

Waiting in San Juan, there was more unrest all over South America so I decided we would withdraw with the aircraft as I had originally suggested. When we arrived in Lima the station manager had some ideas of his own. He said the anti-

British demonstrations were just rent-a-mobs orchestrated by the Argentines. He suggested that we moved to *Hyatt Village* hotel, which was in a quiet area, too far out of town to be troubled by unruly crowds who couldn't afford the bus fare anyway. I was persuaded with this solution.

The *Hyatt Village* is a charming hotel built like a Peruvian village. The rooms were built like cottages set each side of the main street. We spent a quiet, if anxious, week there. The chief steward had a good portable radio that could pick up HF frequencies, so I was able to hear the BBC World Service and keep in touch with events. It was an anxious time. If the Argies managed to sink the carriers with Exocet missiles, it would be all over.

Towards the end of the week the manager of the hotel invited us, and the Lufthansa crew, all to dinner in his top restaurant. Inevitably, the talk got around to the Falklands situation and I found myself unloading my frustrations. The following account may seem lengthy and irrelevant, but I recount it because it may be relevant to what happened after.

I ridiculed the Argentine position that the Malvinas was rightfully theirs because some pope had ceded it to them several hundred years ago. What about the wishes of the people that had lived there for the last 160 years? A country is owned, I proselytized, by the people who inhabit it, by the people who own the houses, own the farms and till the fields. The Falklanders had already indicated democratically, by unanimous vote, that they wanted to stay British. I mentioned that there is little evidence that democracy, the interpretation of the will of the people by free vote is well understood in South America and Argentina in particular with its military dictatorship. I pointed out that the Falklands had been British for longer than Texas and California had been American. Did the Mexicans hope to revert these states by the same Argentine reasoning? If Argentina claimed the Falklands because they were closest, then, by the same token, Alaska belonged to Canada. Did the Argentines have any logical response to such logical argument or did they imagine emotional response was enough? By this time the Lufthansa captain was kicking me under the table, but I wasn't finished yet.

'Finally', I said, 'One of those helicopters is being flown by Prince Andrew. I am not a monarchist myself but the British are funny about their royal family. If Prince Andrew gets shot down and killed, I can assure Argentina that a vendetta will begin that will last a thousand years.'

At this point the dinner was ended. Outside the Lufthansa captain told me he was trying to warn me that the hotel manager was an Argentine and that he was probably on the phone to his ambassador right now. He said he hoped I hadn't stirred up trouble for myself.

We left Lima on schedule and landed in Bogotá. On the turnaround we were about three quarters full, and we loaded freight and fresh flowers in the hold. As we taxied out to the runway the control tower called us up and ordered us to return to the stand.

I knew at once it was a bomb threat; I'd been half expecting something. We were directed to a stand well away from the terminal. The passengers were off-loaded and we began a thorough search of the aircraft.

There must be a million places on an aircraft where you could hide a bomb and the only way to be absolutely sure would be to remove every panel, which is equivalent to a rebuild job and impractical. I ordered all the freight to be off-loaded, knowing full well that the flowers would have to be junked. I figured any person intelligent enough to build a bomb would have calculated an explosion time whilst we were airborne, so I was happy to waste a time equivalent to the next sector time to Caracas, so that if it was a time bomb, it would explode while we were still on the ground.

The crew, the engineers and the police dogs, gave the aircraft a thorough sniffing inside and out. We dropped every panel we, and some bomber, could reasonably get at. With later bomb threats I used to pressurize the aircraft with everything on board except the passengers. Then I would go through a couple of pressurization cycles so that, if the bomb had a pressure sensitive fuse, at least it would go off while we were on the tarmac. I cannot recall if I started this practice in Bogotá that day.

After we had done everything I could think of I noticed that the crew, the police, security and searchers had subsided into little groups on the tarmac. They were talking animatedly together, but the body language indicated they were waiting for something: the next step.

Then came a defining moment for an airline captain. They were waiting for me to decide whether to take the aircraft or not. I had to decide that, either there was a bomb on board and we should dismantle the aircraft until we found it, or that there wasn't a bomb on board and we should reload the aeroplane and continue with our flight. Perhaps for the first time I realized why the pay was so good.

In view of the background security checks that my chief pilot had assured me were already in place, and, in my opinion our searches had been thorough enough to have found any bomb if there had been one on board, I decided we would continue on to Caracas. I had all the passenger's luggage assembled on the tarmac and had all the passengers identify their own luggage. Only these bags were reloaded.

We began our pre-flight routines. I told the passengers on the PA that we had had a bomb threat, that the company had been expecting this kind of disruption and had already been taking stringent precautions. I told them we had thoroughly searched the aircraft with sniffer dogs, that I had off-loaded all the freight and that the only thing in the hold was their own baggage, which they had each identified for themselves.

Then I had one final idea. I asked the passengers, in the circumstances, to think very carefully. Were any of them carrying something for a third party, something that they didn't really know what it was? If they were, now was the time to tell me about it. After a few minutes the chief steward came up and told me that one lady passenger had admitted she was carrying a box of rock samples addressed to the Chemistry Department of Cambridge University on behalf of some students from Bogota's university. I was not at all happy about carrying any package from the chemistry lab of one university to another on behalf of some possibly politically hot-headed South American students, so we opened up the hold again, located the lady's suitcase and the offending package was carried away by security. I was never told, but if there was a bomb on the aircraft, then that was it. If only Captain James MacQuarrie of Panam Flight 103 had been warned about his bomb threat, he would undoubtedly have done exactly the same as me, and the Lockerbie disaster would never have happened.

We flew on to Caracas. We had spent so much time in Bogota that it was now evening. On the approach the control tower informed me that they had had a threat to shoot us down with a SAM (surface-to-air missile). What were my intentions? By this time I was undergoing a sense of humour failure. You can't go into your local supermarket and buy a SAM missile, so frankly I was sceptical. I told them I didn't believe it, and that we would continue the approach.

SAMs are heat-seeking missiles that need to be aimed approximately towards their target, so, in the extremely unlikely event that there actually was a SAM out there, the hit man would have been warned to be careful not to mistake the DC10 with VIASA's own Boeing 727s, as each had an identical three-engine configuration. I knew from experience that it is sometimes very difficult to distinguish between aircraft of a similar engine configuration and particularly so in the gathering gloom of dusk. For example, at distance, the de Havilland Heron is very easy to mistake for the Vickers Viscount, which is more than four times the size. Our possible hit man would have been briefed that the only way to be sure he was aiming at a DC10 would be because it was flashing the high-intensity lights required by the heavy jets. He would have been told to aim at the aircraft with these distinctive flashing high intensity lights, so I switched them off.

We landed okay, turned around and refuelled for San Juan where the next crew were waiting. Just in case our SAM hit man had repositioned himself at the take-off end of the runway, I left the high-intensity lights off until we were passing three thousand feet.

At San Juan I handed over to the next captain who was surprised to see us as our duty day had extended well into 'captain's discretion', meaning I would have to write a violation report for the CAA with my explanation for the excess.

At the Holiday Inn San Juan I mustered the crew in my room for a well-deserved drink on behalf of the company and me. I called down to room service and ordered two bottles of their best champagne, only to be informed that the bar was now closed. Unbelievably, they were not prepared to make any concessions. I will never forgive San Juan nor Holiday Inns for this crass inhospitality. However, we all had our own supplies with us, so we partied a little, but we were all desperately drained, so we soon went to bed.

The next day we positioned to Barbados, where one of the crew knew a couple of hooligans who lived in a villa on the beach with a private pool. So, in Barbados we celebrated, or at least I think so. I can remember objecting to being thrown in the pool because the water would wash out the watermark on the Amex traveller's cheques in my wallet and invalidate them. If that happened they wouldn't get their allowances paid. Crews are very mercenary and my reasoning convinced them. I delegated the throwing in the pool ritual so they threw the co-pilot in instead. (Sorry Dave.)

An interesting footnote to the Falklands conflict is that on my next trip we were slipping in Recife on the North East corner of Brasil while the RAF's Vulcan was making its extremely long-range bombing runs on Stanley Airfield. Our crew party was gate-crashed by some American pilots who said they were in Recife on an exercise. I asked them what they were flying and they said they were flying a tanker; but they were very coy about who they were refuelling in our quiet corner of the South Atlantic.

A few months later I was rostered for a week's slip in the Seychelles on a charter for Air Seychelles. The flight deck positioned to Frankfurt to wait for the aircraft coming out of Heathrow. The cabin staff, with a longer available duty day, would transit with the aircraft. Because we were chartering for Air Seychelles we had to use an Air Seychelles flight number instead of our usual Caledonian prefix. My co-pilot had an extraordinary difficulty with this.

'Frankfurt Tower, this is Caledonian ... correction Air Seychelles Four zero one request start up.'

'Roger Air Seychelles Four zero one, cleared to start.'

'Frankfurt Tower, this is Caledonian ... correction Air Seychelles Four zero one request taxi.'

'Roger Air Seychelles Four zero one, cleared to taxi. Use taxiway Alpha for runway two six.'

In the cockpit, each one of these fluffs was costing my co-pilot a pint of beer, and he was already two pints adrift.

'Frankfurt Tower, this is Caledonian ... correction Air Seychelles Four zero one request take-off.'

'Roger Air Seychelles Four zero one, cleared to take-off. After take-off climb ahead to four thousand feet and contact Frankfurt Approach on One Two Seven decimal three.'

'Roger Tower, Caledonian ... correction Air Seychelles Four zero one is cleared for take-off to climb ahead to four thousand.'

My co-pilot was now up to four pints of beer. After take-off we switched radio channels as directed.

'Frankfurt Approach, this is Caledonian ... correction Air Seychelles Four zero one passing two thousand feet for four thousand.'

'Roger, Caledonian ... correction Air Seychelles Four zero one, you are cleared to climb to flight level three three zero direct to Munich.'

All the way out of Germany, Caledonian ... correction Air Seychelles Four zero one became our call sign. Not a word was spoken, but we could practically feel the tongue in cheek.

Who says the Germans have no sense of humour? By the time we got to the Seychelles my co-pilot owed me a barrel of beer. (I'm still waiting Steve.)

A week in the Seychelles can seem like a long time if you aren't a swimming pool lizard, so it was a relief when HMS *Glamorgan* and *Brazen* arrived. A reconnaissance mission arrived by helicopter and naval intelligence soon established that there were eleven only partially defended air hostesses on the island. A probing party was promptly organized in the *Glamorgan* and the entire Caledonian, correction Air Seychelles, crew were invited on board.

The flight deck were invited by the captain to see the battle control centre where he described to us his Exocet avoidance strategy, which consisted of a carefully timed turn to present the aft, heavily reinforced, gun turret to take the hit if the tinfoil storm failed to confuse the Exocet's homing electronics. In the Falklands War the ship took an Exocet hit, the brunt of which was contained in the galley. The ship, though wounded, was able to continue operations.

The girls disappeared and were not seen again until call-time several days later.

I was particularly interested to hear the captain's opinion about a worrying report that several of our ships had been hit by torpedoes that had failed to explode. This proved to be alarmist journalism and the mysterious thumps experienced by several ships was caused by whales who would use ships to scratch their backs to relieve barnacle irritation in deep water when the bottom was too far away to reach – a very plausible explanation.

At one time BCAL almost achieved a bidline rostering system like most major airlines. Bidline had been agreed and accepted as part of an annual pay deal. My contribution to this was the factorized duty times, whereby all duty would be factorized by the degree of unsocial hours. Night flying between the hours of 1 a.m. and 7 a.m. would be factorized by 2. Evenings between 6 p.m. and 1 a.m. would be factorized by 1.5 as would be Saturdays and Sundays. 7 a.m. to 6 p.m. would have a factor of 1. Using factorized duty times we proposed to offer the company the facility to produce bidlines of absolute maximum efficiency within the Civil Aviation Authority's overriding duty and flying hours' limits provided that overtime was paid for any duty over and above the industry norm of the forty-hour week.

This rationalization caused vertigo in some of the less adaptable members of the PLC and bidline became scuttled. I suspect that the new Flight Operations Director, John Fugl, suddenly realized how much overtime they were getting for free. The vote to drop bidline was nine to one in favour, and in disgust I left the PLC forever.

Mark Young, BALPA's General Secretary, took me to lunch in an attempt at rapprochement but I was adamant that this surrender of the bidline system, which had been agreed with the company as a composite part of a previous pay deal, was such an important decision affecting every pilot's lifestyle and pay packet that, constitutionally, it was a potential pay rise beyond the power of the PLC to just give away; a decision that should have been put to the pilots themselves. In the manner of the mendacious, neither my resignation after sixteen years, nor the reason for it, was even mentioned in the minutes of the meeting.

Two years later we were taken over by BA and everybody took to their bidline system as naturally as ducks to water.

In 1985 my son joined me at the airline. Mark had been extremely unlucky not to have been the right age at the right time in a period of recession and had missed all the easy routes to qualification; such as the excellent pilot's courses at Hamble funded by British Airways. I had helped him with a basic flying course in America but had run out of funds from having to pay back what I had borrowed. By virtue of a single-minded determination, Mark made the grade the hard way – all seven hundred hours' worth. For every pilot who makes it the hard way there are a hundred wannabes who fail. Within and throughout the airline industry there is a special respect for those who set out to scale this particular Everest, and succeed.

In 1988, BCAL was taken over by British Airways. With six years to go before BCAL retirement date I had expected to have enough time to bid for the new Boeing 747-400 Series, but BA imposed their own normal retirement date of fifty-five and I was lucky to get a twenty-month contract while they retrained their co-pilots for my job. The package looked reasonable until the tax was deducted, but, being ejected from our own pension fund made a huge hole in my end of career calculations.

I suppose one cannot blame Lord King and Colin Marshall for not inviting Sir Adam to the British Airways Board; he was a threat. Adam had created a famous international airline out of nothing, something that Lord King was not capable of doing. Sidelining Adam remains an unforgivable slight to the finest man I ever met. It was the sort of insult only a genuine philistine could have perpetrated. I was not alone in my high opinion of Sir Adam Thomson. At his memorial service, St Clement Danes Chapel was so full of BCAL crew and ground staff, the galleries had to be opened to cope with the overflow. Lord King also attended the service and it was whispered amongst the pews that he only came to get his knife back.

I have already mentioned with some pious satisfaction that the airline industry is unique in that it reports and publishes its cock-ups for the safety benefit of the rest of the industry – which leaves me no option but to admit those of my own.

Inevitably, autobiographies are viewed with a rose-tint and I do not wish to leave the reader with the erroneous impression that I was some kind of Biggles. So, hoist by my own petard, I am including some of those decisions I would prefer to have forgotten in the hope that the statute of limitations will protect me from the wrath of the CIA.

On my first job in civil aviation, when I was flying around Blackpool Tower in a Dragon Rapide, Russ Whyham, the parsimonious owner, advised me we had a charter of book-makers to the Newmarket races. It was a welcome task to get out of the circuit and I duly safely delivered the party to the course with a tricky landing because the approach was badly obstructed by trees.

On the ground I grandly instructed Shell Oil to 'fill her up', à la Navy style. The Shell refueller came back to me and said he couldn't find our credit carnet. The reason for this was because we did not have a carnet and the Shell man said I would have to pay in cash (this was before credit cards were invented). Russ Whyham didn't pay me enough money to afford lunch never mind a full tank of gasoline so I had no option but to try and get back to Blackpool with my residual fuel.

I kept a close, even anxious eye on the fuel gauges, which were located on top of the each engine cowling, and as it became night I had to shine a torch on to these gauges. As we got close to Squires Gate I did a lot of shining. Luckily, the bookmaking passengers had had a good day and were too 'tanked up' with a different type of fuel to register my anxiety. We landed with the gauges hovering on empty and I was sweating blood. At the dispersal I don't recall if I shut down the engines or they expired, but I chastised myself for being such a bloody fool and vowed never to repeat the experience.

With the benefit of hindsight, I should have tried to borrow money from the bookies, but the Navy never asks anybody for help and traditionally sorts problems unaided. I thought it would be interesting to find out how much fuel was actually left from the amount required to refill the tanks, but I didn't really want to know.

Many years later, as a newly promoted Boeing 707 captain, we were positioning the aircraft from Niagara Falls to Toronto, a piffling short flight of some twenty-eight miles. With weather of eight-eighths blue we didn't need to refuel the aircraft as we already had residual fuel after our flight from London.

We were cleared to take off and climb to 6,000 feet. The take-off runway allowed a breathtaking view of the falls and before I even had time to call for the after take-off checklist I became horrified to see we were already at 8,000 feet! My voice box could not vibrate fast enough to cope with everything I had to do within the next two seconds and I had to own up and apologise to Niagara that we had violated. Luckily, there was no opposite direction traffic at 7,000 feet and the controller was cool. Everything after went smoothly. I had never before taken off in an absolutely empty Boeing 707 with no passengers and very little fuel and so had never experienced the associated explosive rate of climb more common to Cape Canaveral.

On another transatlantic flight from America to London, we had crossed the coast, got our Atlantic NAT track clearance and were all set when the engineer reported that we seemed to be losing oil from the number three engine oil tank. Dyspeptically we monitored the gauge over the next hour or so and calculated that the oil was not going to last as far as the UK so I made one of those too clever decisions – we would shut the engine down now and then restart at 20 West ready for a normal landing at Gatwick. Since it was only a precautionary shutdown I did not report it to Oceanic Control who would have expected me to turn around and return as we had not yet reached the critical point (the point on a flight where it is equal in time to go forwards or turn around and go back).

The faultiness of this decision was soon apparent. We were not able to maintain our cleared altitude on three engines. When I attempted to restart the engine, the last of its oil emptied with the restart so I had to shut it down again.

The lesson to all pilot readers is how readily one poor decision inevitably leads to others. At this point, BA on the level below overtook us visually underneath.

Since the next aircraft had to be at least twenty minutes behind BA because this was the minimum separation on the Atlantic and if I declared the engine out configuration I would have to turn around and go back, and since we were so very close to critical point, I decided to cheat a little. I let the aircraft drift down a bit of altitude, to recover the height later as we burned off fuel and got lighter. I should have declared the engine out and gone back to the US, but we were so close to the critical point the devil made me do it, but I was seriously bending all the rules.

As luck would have it, my engineer was the same engineer as I had when I overshot my cleared altitude coming out of Niagara Falls so this guy has me down as needing to be NOTAMed (Notices to Airmen) as a danger to navigation. It is usefully humbling to know that, in a whole airline full of highly competent professionals, somebody has you marked down as rubbish.

The last bad decision was more unfortunate than bad. Coming into Gatwick as an experienced pilot, but newly qualified on the BAC 1-11, I was advised by air traffic control that if I could get down to 4,000 feet by 40 miles east of the Golf Echo NDB, I could expect a straight in approach to runway Two-Six; a worthwhile saving of time and fuel.

I looked at the offer and decided it could be done, but only just. My mistake was that if I had still been in a Boeing 707 there would have been no problem. But I was in an unfamiliar BAC 1-11 with a less sophisticated pressurization system, so we got down to 4,000 feet within 40 miles, but for the last 2,000 feet the passenger cabin pressure was overtaken by events and the passengers ears were subjected to a 3,000 feet a minute rate of descent with my co-pilot moaning in anguish. Having agreed we could comply with such a specific and tight mandate there wasn't any time for revisions and reconsiderations; we had to follow through. Nobody's eardrums burst, but it was not my best decision.

To try and restore the reader's plummeting opinion of the author, I conclude with the perfect flight. We were out of LA for Gatwick which was forecasting fog, so I had squeezed out every last ounce of fuel and we were at maximum take-off weight. The skies were busy and we were being held down by traffic, which was eating into my precious excess fuel. By the time we got our Atlantic clearance we still had not got to our most fuel efficient altitude. Then we had a bit of luck, the aircraft above us requested a different track, and surprisingly got it, so I requested his altitude and got that, so at least we were operating ideally.

At 20 West we got the Gatwick weather, and it was completely fogbound. I asked air traffic control, in view of the Gatwick weather we weren't in any hurry and, if approved, we would like to go into holding mode right now. Surprisingly they agreed and we descended 8,000 feet and went into holding mode, which involves consuming the least amount of fuel possible. The difference was that at least it was useful mileage as opposed to just going round in circles in the holding stack.

Gatwick was fogbound as we arrived overhead so we went into the Midhurst holding stack. We worked our way down as traffic below us ran short of fuel and started diverting to Heathrow, which was soon overloaded. Our Operations Department advised us that, if we diverted now we would have to go to Manchester. There were performance manuals all over the cockpit as the flight engineer worked out a new fuel reserve needed to get us to Manchester with the legal minimum. When the fuel got down to 8,800 kilos we had to go to Manchester, which was forecasting reasonable weather. Nobody likes to divert; the passengers get stressed, the aeroplanes are in the wrong place for the next day's programme and a desperately tired crew often has to drive seven hours in a bus to get back to base, and bed.

The Gatwick fog was beginning to show signs of lifting, but the RVR (Runway Visual Range) was variable and still below limits, so, as our fuel began to dwindle down towards the 8,800 kilos, I told air traffic that I would like to make an approach as far as the Outer Marker, which is as close as we could legally go with weather reported below minima. I briefed for the probable overshoot while radar vectored us onto the ILS. Just before we reached the Outer Marker I requested a final RVR check. RVR is given in three sectors along the runway, threshold, middle and far end. We needed 600 yards minimum at the threshold and 600 in the middle. To my surprise it was exactly on the limits, 600/600/100, so we came on in. I saw the approach lights and then the runway, and so, much to our combined surprise, we landed and arrived back to base.

After clearing the runway I asked the flight engineer how much fuel was left.

'8,800 kilos,' he answered.

We had juggled our flight legally, safely, efficiently and even intelligently to the exact kilo. It was a nice moment.

If ever I had a particularly interesting trip I would take my wife and daughter, Tessa, with me. They usually managed to get a first class upgrade if there was space available so they didn't object too much. My daughter was about three on her first trip, and to keep her occupied, my wife had her listening to the music on the in-flight entertainment, which I interrupted to make the usual pre-departure welcome announcement. My daughter whipped off the headphones and stared into the ear piece. 'Daddy, where are you?' she demanded to know, a story that is endlessly recounted in family folklore.

So, on my last trip prior to retirement, I took my family with me and we enjoyed a suite in the *Princess Hotel*, Bermuda. It didn't feel like a last trip until we got back to Gatwick. To my surprise the crew had clubbed together and bought me something that must rate as the most apt goodbye present ever. Somewhere in Bermuda the co-pilot, Paul Roper, had found a clock – a time zone clock with a second hand that was a Boeing 747 going endlessly round the world. Most apt of all was that the clockmaker was called Lord King Quartz. It was so unexpected, I came very close to breaking up, but this clock has been in pride of place on my mantelpiece ever since, and will ever so remain.

Appendix

Retirement brought unexpected realizations, that I had spent my life working amongst some of the most accomplished characters you could possibly hope to meet in a lifetime; quality guys who had themselves managed, successfully, to jump through every hoop a fast developing and demanding job could ask of them. They were winners, every single one of them, and I would like to conclude with a pen portrait of the types I shared a life and career with.

The Techlog is as revered as the bible in aviation circles and is the principal source of contact between the pilots and the engineers who hold each other in high regard as you will note from the following extracts, which are industry standards.

Captain's entry: 'Left inside main tyre almost needs replacement.'

Engineering action: 'Almost replaced left inside main tyre.'

Captain's entry: 'Test flight OK, except autoland very rough.'

Engineering action:	'Autoland not installed on this aircraft.'
Captain's entry:	'Something loose in cockpit.'
Engineering action:	'Something tightened in cockpit.'
Captain's entry:	'Autopilot in altitude-hold mode produces a 200 feet per minute descent.'
Engineering action:	'Unable to reproduce this problem on the ground.'
Captain's entry:	'Evidence of leak on right main landing gear.'
Engineering action:	'Evidence removed.'
Captain's entry:	'DME volume unbelievably loud.'
Engineering action:	'DME volume set to more believable level.'
Captain's entry:	'Friction locks cause throttle levers to stick.'
Engineering action:	'That's what they're there for.'
Captain's entry:	'IFF inoperative.'
Engineering action:	'IFF always inoperative in OFF mode.'
Captain's entry:	'Suspected crack in windshield.'
Engineering action:	'Suspect you're right.'
Captain's entry:	'Number 3 engine missing.'
Engineering action:	'Number 3 engine found on right wing after brief search.'

Another group of aeronautical workers in awe of pilots are the air traffic controllers.

Air traffic controllers are would-be pilots who just weren't handsome enough, so they stuck them in a darkened room where they are heard but never seen. All they do all day is talk so inevitably they get quite good at it. It is unwise to bandy words with an air traffic controller as you are likely to suffer ego damage.

Pilot:	'Tower, give me a rough time-check!'
Tower:	'Certainly, sir. It's Tuesday.'
Tower:	'Alpha Tango, do you intend to land or what?'
Pilot:	'Yes.'
Tower:	'Yes what?'
Pilot:	'Yes, *sir*!'
Pilot:	'Tower, please call me a fuel truck.'
Tower:	'With pleasure, sir. You are a bowser.'
Pilot:	'Good morning, Frankfurt ground, KLM 242 request start up and push back.'
Tower:	'KLM 242 expect start up in two hours.'
Pilot:	'Please confirm: two hours delay?'
Tower:	'Affirmative.'
Pilot:	'In that case, cancel the good morning!'

During a twenty aircraft take-off queue at Kennedy:

Pilot:	'Kennedy, I'm fucking bored with this.'
Kennedy:	'Would the aircraft reporting boredom please identify yourself.'
Pilot:	'I said I was fucking bored, not fucking stupid'

After landing the crew of a heavy jet made a wrong turn during taxi and came nose to nose with another outbound aircraft. The furious female ground controller screamed:

'Oscar Papa, where do you think you are going? I told you to turn right on 'Charlie' taxiway; you turned right on 'Delta'. Stop right there.'

There was an embarrassed silence.

'Oscar Papa, you've screwed up everything. It will take forever to sort this out. You stay right there and don't move until I tell you to. You can expect progressive taxi instructions in about half an hour and I want you to go exactly where I tell you, when I tell you, and how I tell you. You got that?'

After a few seconds of deathly hush an unknown voice said,

'Ma'am, wasn't I married to you once?'

| Shannon Tower: | 'Shamrock 123, what is your height and position?' |
| Shamrock 123: | 'I'm five foot eight and sitting in the pilot's seat.' |

A unique feature of Navy aircraft is their ability to fold their wings for tight stowage on space-limited aircraft carriers.

Navy 35:	'Navy 35, request take-off.'
Tower:	'Navy 35 negative take-off.'
	(Time passes.)
Navy 35:	'Tower, request take-off.'
Tower:	'Navy 35, negative take-off.'
	(More time passes.)
Navy 35:	'Navy 35, request take-off.'
Tower:	'Negative take-off Navy 35.'
Navy 35:	'Tower, can you give me some idea when I'll get take-off clearance?'
Tower:	'Roger, Navy 35. You can take off as soon as you've spread your wings.'

Perhaps my favourite is a DC10 that landed going very fast and was braking so desperately that the tyres were billowing smoke, highlighting the pilot's anxiety for the entire airport to see.

San Jose Tower: 'American 751 heavy, turn right at the end of the runway – if able. If not able, take the Guadeloupe exit off of Highway 101, make a right turn at the lights and follow the signposts back to Terminal 3.'

I never realized how much I was going to miss the quality until I wasn't there. I am frequently asked if I miss flying and the answer is yes and no. It occurs to me now that I had spent thirty-five years of my life being only one moment of carelessness away from disaster; just one moment's inattention to detail; just one moment of inadequacy or stupidity and this whole account could have been post-humous; and that is the synthesis of an airline pilot's life, and why a policy of correcting your mistakes before they happen is what being a good pilot is all about. So paradoxically I miss the pressure, of needing to be one hundred percent always 'on-the-ball'.

The future?

I have seen aircraft grow from the thirty-six-seat DC3 to the 800-seat giants of today. I have seen radio operators being replaced by HF radio, navigators replaced by inertial navigation systems of amazing accuracy and reliability, flight engineers replaced by foolproof automatic systems that even dumb pilots can handle. Already, we have a blind landing system that can land in a fog where a pilot can't even see the ground. I met a BAE boffin who boasted they already had technology that could replace pilots altogether.

We are now flying aircraft where the control column is not connected to the control surfaces except via a computer, and the thrust levers are not connected to the engines except via a computer. Inevitably, over the next century we will see aircraft with a single pilot having just a monitoring role in the cockpit. I have already said that I have no trouble flying as a passenger today because I know how safe the whole system is, but no pilot at all?

It is certain in life that you can always expect one thing, that one day the unexpected will happen. It would be a pretty remarkable computer driven by an even more remarkable programme to assess, after a double engine failure after take-off caused by bird-strike ingestion, that the best option available was to ditch in the River Hudson. So, speaking as a passenger, I think I would not feel very comfortable unless I knew there was somebody like a Captain Sullenberger in the cockpit.